HEARTFELT ADVICE

Heartfelt Advice

Lama Dudjom Dorjee

SNOW LION PUBLICATIONS
ITHACA, NEW YORK

Snow Lion Publications
P. O. Box 6483
Ithaca, NY 14851 USA
(607) 273-8519
www.snowlionpub.com

Printed in USA on acid-free recycled paper.

ISBN-10: 1-55939-346-7
ISBN-13: 978-1-55939-346-1

Library of Congress Cataloging-in-Publication Data

Dudjom Dorjee, Lama.
  Heartfelt advice / Lama Dudjom Dorjee.
    p. cm.
  ISBN-13: 978-1-55939-346-1 (alk. paper)
  ISBN-10: 1-55939-346-7 (alk. paper)
  1. Buddhism—China—Tibet. 2. Buddhism—
Doctrines. I. Title.
BQ7612.D83 2010
294.3'420423—dc22

                                    2009036837

Designed and typeset by Gopa & Ted2, Inc.

✂ Table of Contents

❦ Introduction

This book contains exactly what the title promises: the heart-felt advice of our precious lama, Khenpo Dudjom Dorjee Rinpoche, to his spiritual friends, the students of the buddha dharma. As such, *Heartfelt Advice* is not necessarily intended to be used in the traditional Western manner of reading from cover to cover, start to finish, from page one to the end. Rather, think of it more as a user's guide or daily devotional tract in that you may glance through the table of contents or even simply flip the pages of the book until you see one of the ninety-five titles that interests you or addresses your spiritual needs at that time. The individual short chapters are not ordered in any way that would require reading the preceding chapters as a prerequisite for understanding those that follow. In fact, each one has it's own individual life and energy to benefit the student, independently of any of the others. It will bring to your study of the dharma a blend of compassion and wisdom that we always see from the realized masters of the Vajrayana: their ability to give us less of what we want, and more of what we need. Whether he is delivering the sometimes unpleasant or uncomfortable truths of suffering from the Hinayana, the boundless compassion of the Mahayana, or the radiant wisdom and bliss of the Vajrayana, Rinpoche holds nothing back.

Heartfelt Advice was written during a period from the winter of 2006 to the winter of 2007. It was very much inspired by the teachings contained within a Tibetan text that is a collection from the original sutra and tantra teachings of the historical Buddha as well as other great masters from the history of

Buddhism. During short daily sessions, Rinpoche would read to me from the original text in Tibetan and then, as I do not speak any Tibetan, he would translate the short verses that he had read. He would also give me his own commentary on those original writings based on his understanding and realization, cultivated from over three decades of studying, practicing, and teaching the buddha dharma. The short chapters you see here in this book are a record (read, corrected, and approved by Rinpoche) of my own understandings of those priceless conversations.

Aaron Price
Dallas, Texas
April 2008

My Prayer for the End of Suffering

May this offering of prayer please the buddhas and bodhisattvas of the three times and ten directions, in order to free every sentient being from all bonds of suffering and dualistic experience in samsara.

May it please the yidams and dharmapalas, those great beings that have within their power the ability to guide and protect all dharma practitioners in the human realm.

May this prayer offering satisfy the needs and desires of all beings within the six realms of samsara, thereby being the cause of attainment of the ultimate goal, liberation from the bondage of pain and suffering.

May this practice of generously offering up my prayers bring purification of the negative karma born from countless debts and failures of responsibilities.

May this prayer repay all my debts, accrued from beginningless time, and satisfy all responsibilities to my fellow beings of the six realms, being the cause of liberation from the bondage of suffering in samsara.

May this immeasurably generous offering of prayer bring all beings, without exception, limitless freedom, great resources, and material abundance.

May this prayer bring the growth of all beings' wisdom and compassion and, through that compassionate wisdom, may they experience the cause of the truest happiness, which is liberation from the pain and suffering of samsara and enlightenment for the benefit of all beings.

Lama D. Dorjee
Dallas, Texas
May 2008

Prologue

One day, during my time at Sanskrit University, His Holiness the Sixteenth Gyalwang Karmapa was passing through nearby Varanasi on a pilgrimage of holy sites. Since he was so close, he stopped to offer blessings to the students of Sanskrit University. This was big news to the community around Varanasi and there was a huge gathering of people, alive with excitement and anticipation.

I got in line with the few spare rupees I had and a khata offering scarf. His Holiness was giving the blessings from his car and the long line of students filed past one by one. As my turn came, I approached with a reverent bow and made my offering, and was astounded when His Holiness gestured for me to step closer to him. When I did, His Holiness spoke to me: "Come up."

All I could do was nod my head in agreement. In fact, I wasn't certain that I hadn't just imagined it. As I stepped away, I stood somewhat to the side and watched the other students approach. I wanted to see if His Holiness was speaking to everyone. But I watched as one, two, three, four and more students passed by, and His Holiness didn't utter a word to any of them. What did it mean? When I later mentioned it to some close friends they told me that it surely meant I should go to His Holiness's monastery in the mountains of Sikkim which, after all, was "up" in the mountains. I was intrigued, but Varanasi was far away from Sikkim, and I was so busy and focused on my university studies. It didn't seem like the right moment to act on it, so I just let the invitation rest in the back of my mind.

• • •

Upon completion of my studies at Sanskrit University, I earned the Acharya Degree and entered the traditional three-year, three-month retreat under the retreat masters His Eminence Beru Kyentse Rinpoche and His Eminence Kyabgon Kalu Rinpoche. The many experiences and dreams I had during three-year retreat contained important messages for me, but when I had completed my retreat I still wasn't completely sure what to do. His Eminence Kyentse Rinpoche's monastery offered me a position as abbot, but my heart told me to enter another three-year retreat. After all, it had been the best and most wonderful time of my life, and deepening my peace and wisdom even more felt like a valid and skillful thing to do. In the three years of retreat, my retreat mates and I had devoted ourselves completely to spiritual development, not creating any negative karma through body, speech, or mind. I'd had the auspicious fortune to receive teachings, guidance, and empowerments from realized masters. Also, I had been extremely inspired by the great practitioners I had met—many who were devoted to twenty-year, thirty-year, or even lifetime retreats. These weren't the yogis of some legend, but great beings with whom I had actually studied and practiced. But, since my father had died, I was eager to make the journey to South India to be with my mother and family.

. . .

I traveled to South India and arrived at my mother's, and while I was there, we had lunch with my family's long-time lama, the Venerable Bakyou Rinpoche, who mentioned casually that His Holiness Karmapa was about to begin a summer retreat at his monastery in Sikkim. Immediately, my mind shot back to the enigmatic invitation I'd received from His Holiness Karmapa seven years earlier. It didn't take me long to sense that there was something auspicious about Rinpoche mentioning the retreat, and that now was the time to complete the puzzle of the invitation and to travel to Rumtek.

I was so determined and enlivened by my decision that I didn't even bother applying for a passport so that I could legally pass into Sikkim. That would have taken much too long. Instead, I left almost immediately, traveling by bus and train from South India all the way to Sikkim with a single handbag. I wore a Karmapa badge on my shoulder and sat quietly. The problem was that the bus passed through two checkpoints between India and Sikkim. At the first checkpoint, the guard walked up and down the aisle checking passports. I was a little nervous. How would I convince him to let me stay on board without a passport? Yet, miraculously, somehow the guard didn't even see me. He simply walked on by.

At the next checkpoint, the guards started through the bus again. I wondered if I could make myself invisible again. This time a guard did approach me, but I think he must have noticed my Karmapa badge, because he asked me in Nepalese, "Are you from Rumtek?" Now, if I were to answer, he would have immediately heard my strange accent (since I didn't speak Nepalese) and realize that I was a foreigner and demand to see my passport, so I simply nodded my head and showed my teeth with a nice big smile. Satisfied, the guard passed on without asking for my passport. I was on my way to Gangtok, the capital of Sikkim.

. . .

When I arrived in Gangtok I met up with some relatives of Bakyou Rinpoche. They welcomed me warmly when I explained my situation and connection to Rinpoche. My good fortune seemed to be coming in bunches: it just so happened that the very day after I arrived they were headed to His Holiness Karmapa's monastery for his birthday celebration. I would be able to travel with them.

After some travel in the car, we reached the mountain on which Rumtek Monastery sits so majestically and began zigzagging our way up the narrow mountain road. We were taking it nice and slow, when suddenly we heard sirens and commotion behind us. A whole parade of VIPs was right behind us, on their way up to His Holiness Karmapa's birthday celebration. Unfortunately, the road was much too narrow for us to let them pass, so we just continued on, leading the procession.

The scene as we approached the monastery was a marvel. Beginning about a quarter-mile from the front gates, monks lined the road. As soon as our car was in sight, they began to play traditional auspicious welcoming music. We made our way along the rows of monks and through the gates. The car pulled up into the courtyard of the monastery, stopped, and some monks came and opened my door for me (though they stepped away and moved on to the next car when they saw we weren't VIPs). As I stepped out of the car, I glanced up and saw His Holiness Karmapa and his entire entourage above on the balcony welcoming the arrivals as well. Standing in front of Rumtek in the midst of such auspicious circumstances, with the music and the monks and high-ranking lamas, and His Holiness himself present, was like a powerful ray of sunlight shooting through me. The beauty of this moment is alive in me to this day. Of course they had mistaken us at that point for VIP guests—like high government officials or something—but the welcome nonetheless had an important effect on me. This special coincidence left an impression on my heart-mind and marks an important event on my spiritual journey.

Before I left South India my mother said she had a nephew in Rumtek who might be able to help me once I got there. So, as soon as all the guests and VIPs from the parade of cars made it into the monastery, I began to ask for my mother's nephew, the Venerable Trinley Parjur. Some monks went in and brought out a very round and shiny-headed but handsome lama. He shook my hand, and said a few things that showed he had already heard a bit about my studies and practice. He was tutor to a tulku at the monastery—the Venerable Trurum Gyaltrul Rinpoche. He invited me to his room, where we sat to have tea with the tulku and talk. Not far into our conversation we heard the gong ring throughout the monastery—it was time to enter the main shrine for darshan (receiving of blessings) with His Holiness Karmapa on his birthday.

I immediately joined the thousands of people who were lined up to approach the Karmapa's high throne to make offerings and receive blessings. Just like seven years before, I patiently followed the line as this long string of people made its way past His Holiness. Little by little the line grew shorter and I got closer and closer to His Holiness.

And, also like seven years before, something quite unexpected happened as I approached His Holiness Karmapa. I was under his throne, making my offering, and to my astonishment, he bent down from his high seat and spoke to me once again! "Have any trouble on the way up?" His Holiness had a serene smile on his face. I smiled and replied, "No, sir!"

Once again, I stood for a moment off to the side to watch and see if His Holiness was talking to everyone. He wasn't. I confess that for a moment my ego was inflated by this unique treatment. But on a deeper level, in my heart, I felt as though His Holiness had been guiding and watching me with his omniscient eye the entire journey.

. . .

After the birthday celebration in the main shrine, I was having tea again back in Venerable Trinley Parjur's room. Out of the blue, one of His Holiness Karmapa's attendants approached me. "Are you the new lama who has just arrived?" he asked. "His Holiness demands that you enter the Summer Retreat right away."

The retreat had begun three days earlier and it was not customary—in fact it was unheard of—for anyone to be admitted late. Nonetheless, under such a request from His Holiness, I couldn't refuse. I told the attendant I was honored and humbly accepted.

Not long after this encounter I heard the gongs and ritual music calling the retreatants back into session. Since I was now a participant, I approached the main shrine room. Just as I was approaching the main door of the monastery, set to enter the retreat, the Summer Retreat's head disciplinarian monk appeared from nowhere and took me by the hand. He walked me into the shrine room, right past all the seats occupied by regular monks, and led me directly to a seat among the high-ranking Rinpoches and tulkus. Realizing what a rare and precious privilege and honor this was, I could only think to myself, "I don't deserve this."

. . .

A few hours into that first session, His Holiness Karmapa's attendant approached me once again and told me His Holiness wished to see me right away. Of course, I happily followed as he led me to the Karmapa's private interview room. When I entered, His Holiness was seated. I offered three prostrations and sat on the floor in front of him.

His Holiness began to speak: "I'm glad you came," he said. "I would like you to enter the Summer Retreat. While you are here you will be treated like a Rinpoche, so please take your meals from the Rinpoche's kitchen. Also, I would like you to come see me every day, and I want you to make a connection with the four regents of the Kagyu lineage."

His Holiness went on to tell me about some other very specific things I was to do while I was there. First, I was to give classes to the younger monks at the monastery. Second, His Holiness seemed to know I had studied Sanskrit, because he asked me to give a lecture (on Sanskrit) to the whole monastery at the conclusion of Summer Retreat. It was a tradition for the most learned and accomplished monks and lamas at Summer Retreat to display their wisdom by giving lectures throughout the night.

Of course I was completely humbled and startled by such orders from His Holiness. He seemed to have the idea or knowledge that my being there with him at Summer Retreat was very important. And being there in his presence, I too could sense a special importance in this time. I had complete faith in his wisdom, and obediently accepted his every request.

I entered the Summer Retreat and visited His Holiness every day. Our interviews were full of teaching, smiling and laughing, and meditating. To me, every single meeting with His Holiness was a precious and momentous event in itself. Every word, gesture, glance, and breath of His Holiness was a transmission of blessings from the Karma Kagyu lineage.

. . .

There are a few of my daily meetings with His Holiness that stand out as quite extraordinary. Once, I was called hastily to His Holiness's chamber. A large group of Westerners was visiting and he had chosen me to be the English translator. I had studied a little bit of English, but by no means was I prepared to translate! But I entered the chamber and took a seat below His Holiness. As the interview began the most miraculous thing happened. Not only could I understand perfectly what the Westerners were saying, but when it came time for me to speak in English the words seemed to flow seamlessly right through me, the Tibetan His Holiness had spoken simply transforming into the English I was speaking to the Westerners. Somehow the blessings of His Holiness temporarily improved my English. Even today, after years living in the United States, I haven't quite returned to that level of proficiency! His Holiness was very pleased after that interview. In fact, I even remember him patting me on the shoulder and saying to his regular translators, who had been watching the whole time, "Now that's how a translator should be!"

As the end of Summer Retreat approached the time came for me to give the lecture on Sanskrit that His Holiness had requested. To make the occasion of the talk even more auspicious, I was asked to give part of the lecture in Sanskrit. Hearing Sanskrit spoken aloud is uniquely auspicious because it was the language of the Buddha Shakyamuni's original teachings, and is often considered a "language of gods."

As I began my talk, the monastery was jam-packed with monks and lamas. Outside, the local Buddhist community was gathered to hear the talks from loudspeakers. When my name was called I was very nervous and excited—honored to have such an opportunity in the presence of His Holiness. I approached the front, gave three slow and careful prostrations, and began to speak. I was taking my speech very seriously, enunciating clearly and projecting my voice out over the large space. All was going wonderfully until I began the part in which I was to speak in Sanskrit. The thing is that most people—even the monks and lamas—had never heard Sanskrit spoken aloud before, and certainly never with the proper accent. When I began to speak Sanskrit the whole monastery erupted in laughter. The lamas were cracking up. The visitors outside were in stitches. Even the disciplinarian monks had lost it. This strange language, when pronounced properly, was so foreign to them that hearing it caused them to break down into hysterical fits of laughter!

Unfortunately, in my serious frame of mind, I took all this laughter the wrong way. It actually made me a bit angry, and I began to raise my voice even louder. This, of course, only roused my audience more. The roars of laughter continued no matter how loud and clear I made my voice. I looked over at His Eminence Jamgon Kongtrul Rinpoche, who was sitting on the high throne, and even he was laughing, but he was also giving me a thumbs-up sign. Finally, as I neared the end of my speech, I noticed His Holiness Karmapa smiling and looking pleased. Up until that moment I was quite upset and bewildered, but my irritation vanished at seeing His Holiness's reaction to my speech.

The next morning, while out circumambulating the holy sites, I found I had become a bit of an instant celebrity with the locals, who had been listening to my speech through the loudspeakers. Apparently, they had enjoyed it as much as all the lamas within the monastery. They told me how impressed they were and invited me for food and drinks. Of course by this time my frustration had subsided and I was grateful for their appreciation.

. . .

Over the course of the forty-five-day Summer Retreat, it had become routine for me to visit His Holiness Karmapa, receiving darshan, teachings, or simply meditating together. One day before Summer Retreat concluded, His Holiness called me to his chambers for a much more unusual audience. I figured this would be like any other of our daily interviews, but when I entered there were several prestigious lamas and eminences present. I scanned the room and noticed a small, decorated throne had been set up right next to His Holiness. I made my three prostrations and sat in my regular spot on the floor, but suddenly all the lamas present began signaling for me to go sit on the small throne. I felt uneasy about taking such a high seat in the presence of His Holiness, so instead of sitting on the throne, I scooted a few feet closer to His Holiness, hoping that would appease them. But again they signaled for me to sit on the throne, so I had no choice. When I was settled, His Holiness ordered tea and cookies. He asked me to make a tea offering, and this moment quickly became a hasty enthrone-ment ceremony. When I was finished he made a gesture to his General Secretary, who began to address me: "His Holiness would like you to represent him in the West." He went on to explain that this was an extremely important request that I certainly shouldn't refuse.

Of course I was a bit surprised, and I hesitated slightly for a couple of reasons. First, I guess I still had the idea or intention that I should enter a second three-year retreat, and then teach and work for the lineage in India. Second, once before, years earlier while I was studying at Sanskrit University, someone had invited me to France. When I approached my mother about that invitation, she had disapproved very strongly. This gave me some doubts about how she would take a second re-quest about going to the West. I didn't want to disrespect the wisdom of His Holiness, or express doubts in the presence of his entourage, but I also needed to clarify my hesitations.

"Your Holiness, you have great wisdom and compassion,

and if you can see a benefit to sentient beings from this, I will do as you ask. However, I'm a little worried that my mother will not approve, and that she won't allow me to go."

"I will handle your mother!" His Holiness exclaimed. "I know she will let you go." At this, he ordered several gifts to be prepared and brought for my mother. I knew without a doubt that it was Karmapa's great wisdom, not the gifts, that would convince my mother, and I accepted my new role as a representative for His Holiness and the Kagyu lineage in the West.

At this point, His Holiness turned to the eminences and began to speak to them of my special qualities, and why I would be an excellent help to the lineage by turning the wheel of dharma in the West. "If he can't do it, no one can!" I could only sit and listen in silence, overcome with gratitude and humility for His Holiness's generous words.

Sure enough, later when I delivered the news and gifts to my mother in South India, she responded with great grace and compassion. "I will let you go if His Holiness sees it is best. Even though it means I will not see you much in this lifetime, I have complete faith in His Holiness." By 1981 I had arrived in New York City to begin my coast-to-coast adventure of living and turning the wheel of dharma in the West. It was also in that year that His Holiness the Sixteenth Gyalwang Karmapa, Rangjung Rigpe Dorje, died in Zion, Illinois, leaving all sentient beings eagerly awaiting his return as the Seventeenth Karmapa.

. . .

Shortly after the Seventeenth Gyalwang Karmapa, Ogyen Trinley Dorje, had been identified, I was able to visit Tsurphu, the main seat and monastery of the Karmapa lineage, with a group of my own students that I had brought with me from the United States. We were very fortunate to have darshan with His Holiness and receive his blessing in this holy place. In the presence of His Holiness the Seventeenth Karmapa, I felt immediately that he was the reincarnation of the Sixteenth Karmapa. He welcomed me just as his predecessor would have, and his features and mannerisms reminded me of the Sixteenth Karmapa. He gave us blessings and transmissions and, although he was a young child, he displayed great confidence and wisdom. Whatever doubts many of my students had previously held about the authenticity of the Seventeenth Karmapa melted away in the presence of the young Ogyen Trinley Dorje.

1.1 Stepping onto the Beginner's Path

In order for us to take our first steps as beginners on the path of liberation, we must have a full understanding of the nature of samsaric experience and the root of its very existence. Simply knowing that we are sick isn't enough to heal us; we must also know the cause of our ailment so that we can take the right medicine to be cured. We should begin by engaging in dharma practice, reducing our involvement in meaningless and harmful activities, including worldly dharmas such as spiritual materialism. As well, we should cultivate a sense of contentment with whatever material wealth we already have. Also, to gain the full benefit of dharma teachings and practice, we must focus inward, using contemplation and meditation to reduce our own ego-clinging, desire, and attachment, as well as increase our own humility and respect toward others. The more we practice dharma, the more our faith and devotion will increase. This is crucial, for we must practice with faith and devotion since they play a key role in our level of connection to the buddha dharma and the attainments that are the result of our dharma practice. We must use this increased level of faith and devotion to further open our hearts and minds to whatever universal knowledge and wisdom will benefit us and our practice.

These are the important steps we must take to have both feet firmly planted on the beginner's path.

1.2 Three Vehicles of Dharma Teachings

Buddha Shakyamuni turned the wheel of dharma three times, leaving us with the three vehicles of teachings, in order to benefit beings of three different levels of development and maturity. All eighty-four thousand of Lord Buddha's teachings fall within one of these three vehicles, which are categorized as Hinayana, Mahayana, and Vajrayana.

The Hinayana, or Lesser Vehicle, is focused on self-liberation through living a wholesome life in accordance with the Buddha's first teaching on the Four Noble Truths. These deal primarily with the truth of suffering and the cessation of suffering.

The Mahayana, or Greater Vehicle, is focused on the fact that self-liberation can only be attained through working for the enlightenment of all sentient beings, without exception, through the practice of the six paramitas, or six perfections. It is only by attaining and maintaining this indiscriminate altruistic outlook, known as bodhichitta, that we can attain the means to achieve enlightenment.

The Vajrayana, or Indestructible Vehicle, is characterized by the view of the inseparability of the practitioner and his or her buddha nature. The Vajrayana allows for the achievement of buddhahood within a single lifetime through practices which focus on the inseparability of the lama and yidam. This intense path is entirely dependent upon the cultivation of a sacred outlook, in which the practitioner comes to view the ordinary body as the body of the enlightened meditational deity, all ordinary speech as the mantra speech of the deity, and the ordinary mind as the enlightened mind of the deity.

You can think of the three yanas, or three vehicles, as the

stages of a new moon that waxes night after night until it has reached the brilliance of the full moon that lights the night. In that sense, the practitioner should value and respect all three vehicles equally in order to obtain buddhahood.

1.3 Discriminating Right and Wrong Paths

An essential aspect of our journey toward liberation is being able to discriminate between right and wrong paths. In short, we must follow the path of the great bodhisattvas and avoid falling onto the paths of samsara.

To follow a right path, we must practice the three yanas of the sacred doctrine of the buddha dharma. This includes utilizing deity visualization practices without any reservations and without cultivating attachment to those practices. From the ultimate point of view, we must practice beyond the notions of conditional and nonconditional, not allowing ourselves to fall into the extremes of existence and nonexistence. Yet from a relative point of view, we must follow the path of the bodhisattva and continue to practice behavior consistent with the altruistic mind, which ultimately leads us to liberation. Even from the Hinayana point of view we must follow the right path of renunciation of and detachment towards samsara so that we may attain the state of an arhat.

In the end, choosing and committing to a right path, whether it be Hinayana, Mahayana, or Vajrayana, rather than a wrong path or no path at all, will determine the results that are produced by our practice.

1.4 The Significance of Taking Refuge

From the external point of view, taking refuge is receiving permission to enter the mandala of Buddhism, of being accepted into the global sangha of practitioners of buddha dharma. Internally, taking refuge allows us to receive the transmissions and blessings of the ultimate Buddha, thus propelling us along the path towards liberation.

When the Buddha appears in the universe, the dharma teachings and the sangha of practitioners also appear. Taking refuge in these three aspects means crossing the dividing line between Buddhist and non-Buddhist—to formally declare it, so to speak. When we take refuge, we, as the subject, go to the object, the Three Jewels—the Buddha, the dharma, and the sangha—for that refuge.

First, we take refuge in the historical Buddha Shakyamuni, as well as in all the buddhas of the three times (past, present, and future) and in the three kayas (dharmakaya, sambhogakaya, and nirmanakaya)—the manifestations of the three bodies of the Buddha. Second, we also take refuge in the holy dharma, in the direct teachings of the Buddha, including all three levels of those teachings (Hinayana, Mahayana, and Vajrayana). Third, we take refuge in the noble sangha, the community of beings with highly developed wisdom and compassion, including arhats and other highly realized practitioners, as well as buddhas and bodhisattvas.

Finally, although we initially see these Three Jewels as separate objects in our practice, from the ultimate point of view we must consolidate them into one single object of refuge—the ultimate Buddha.

1.5 Taking Refuge in the Three Roots

In addition to taking refuge in the Three Jewels, Vajrayana practitioners take refuge in the Three Roots—the lama, the yidams, and the dharma protectors. We take refuge in the first root, the lama, as a being who possesses supreme realizations, and someone that we can rely upon for instruction in dharma practice.

We take refuge in the second root, the yidam deities, because we rely upon their transmissions and blessings to progress along the tantric path.

We take refuge in the third root, the dharma protectors, because we rely upon the protection of their blessings as we continue along the Vajrayana path.

We don't only take refuge in these Three Roots, we actually consolidate them into one—our root lama, or "root guru." When we have a genuine guru whom we see as the embodiment of the Buddha himself, then we also have yidam deities and dharma protectors and all their blessings and protections. When we have the ultimate view of our guru as a buddha, we have the Vajrayana.

1.6 The Essence of the Doctrine

When a doctor makes a diagnosis of a specific disease to a patient, she prescribes a specific medicine which, if taken in the right amounts and at the right times by the patient, will eventually cure the disease. At the point the disease is cured, the medicine becomes unnecessary. This is the essence of the doctrine of the buddha dharma—when certain kleshas and afflictive emotions are identified and the specific practices are applied as an antidote for these poisons, eventually these negativities are overcome and liberation from suffering is attained.

For instance, when we encounter negative emotions, the confused mind perceives no separation between itself and the emotion: the two become conflated and suffering is perpetuated without interruption. However, the skillful mind perceives the negative emotion as separate from the mind itself, that it represents the mere appearance of a dependently-arisen phenomenon empty of any inherent existence.

In order to dig up the root of afflictive emotions the practitioner must first learn the essence of Hinayana doctrines. No matter how many times we cut down a tree, if the root remains below the surface, the tree will grow back the following spring. The same principle holds true for the tree of negative emotions: no matter how much we engage in dharma practice to remove the appearance of negativities, as soon as the causes and conditions come together once again, like the sun and rain that nurture the roots, the afflictive emotions will reappear. Thus, the skillful practitioner must learn the essence of the doctrines of the Hinayana path in order to dig up the very root of these negativities.

To actually use these negative afflictive emotions as fuel for our practice and bring them onto the bodhisattva path we must learn the essence of the Mahayana point of view, which welcomes all difficult or painful experiences as opportunities to expand our practice.

Finally, from the Vajrayana point of view, we can actually transform these kleshas into the wisdom of the Vajrayana practice itself. This is possible as the afflictive emotions are recognized for what they truly are, when their basic nature of perfect purity is understood beyond conceptualization.

1.7 Fear in the Six Realms

Regardless of which of the six realms we enter, they are all bound by the fear of their inherent pain and suffering. Until our accumulated negative karma is exhausted, the fear of suffering and pain will not disappear. Even the happiness and great pleasure experienced by the sentient beings that inhabit the god realm are temporary. Due to this state of impermanence, these beings that live temporarily as gods experience terrible fear the moment they realize that the positive karma they've accumulated from previous virtuous actions has begun to run out and their descent back into the lower realms has begun.

Due to the positive karma that has brought them to their higher level of existence in the god realm, beings there have the ability to see seven days ahead of time which realm of samsara they will be falling into next, and the fear that their unimaginably pleasurable existence is about to end is compounded by the clear view they have of the suffering they will experience in the lower realms in the future.

In the demigod realm beings experience terrible fear due to their constant state of warfare; they are perpetually locked in battle with their foes, destroying each other in combat.

Here in the human realm we experience suffering from our fear of old age, sickness, and death. Due to our own accumulation of negative karma, birth in the human realm creates for us an existence in which these three types of suffering are unavoidable. Although the human realm is the best realm from which to attain liberation from the cycle of samsara, if we fail to practice virtuous action in this life, our suffering will continue because we'll remain trapped within the six realms.

In the animal realm beings experience the constant fear and tension of not knowing where they will get their next meal, as well as the fear of being eaten as someone else's next meal! Sure, animals don't speak our language, and they seem to have dull minds, but that does not mean they do not experience great fear as a result of their samsaric experience (that is, the constant threat of being eaten by another).

The preta realm is inhabited by hungry ghosts that constantly experience great suffering from the fear of starving to death or dying of thirst due to their previous life's greed and lack of virtuous acts, such as generosity.

In the hell realms beings experience unbelievable extremes of scorching heat and freezing cold as a result of the negative karma accumulated through their acts of terrible anger, hatred, aggression, and violence toward other sentient beings.

We see from this overview of the suffering experienced in each of the six realms that, until we have not only purified the negative karma accumulated from past actions but also cleansed ourselves of all negative emotions which cause us to act in negative ways and plant even more seeds of negative karma, we will remain locked in this cycle of inescapable suffering and fear.

It's true that, relatively speaking, some realms and their particular conditions are better than others, but as long as we exist within the six realms of samsara we live in the constant fear of their inevitable suffering.

1.8 Attachment to the Physical Body

Generally speaking, we ordinary human beings are extremely attached to our own physical bodies. When we analyze this physical body to which we are so attached, we see that it is composed of four basic elements: fire, water, earth, and air. Yet when we analyze these constituent parts of our physical existence in turn, we cannot find anything special, anything that is worth being attached to.

What we do find is a collection of over two hundred bones, various muscle groups, organs, and skin which, when laid out in pieces across a dissection table, are not attractive in the least. Imagine that without our outer covering of skin and flesh all the bones, or the skeleton inside, would be laid bare for all to see—quite an uncomfortable and unpleasant sight. Not to mention all the liquids of which our body is composed: blood, mucus, bile, partially digested food, as well as urine and other excrement. These are beyond "unattractive"—they are outright disgusting to witness in their raw form and certainly not worth the attachment most humans display toward them through attachment to their bodies!

This human body we possess is both home and food for millions of other sentient beings such as bacteria, viruses, and parasites who don't see us as anything special, but merely a habitat they share with countless other inhabitants. In fact, this human body naturally attracts a wide variety of diseases that cause the suffering of sickness we experience when it is thrown out of balance.

So when we examine our physical bodies and their constituent parts it should become easy to detach ourselves from our physical existence and see it simply as a means to an end,

1.9 Illusion and Impermanence

Everything that appears depends on causes and conditions for its existence; therefore, anything that begins in creation must end in decay and destruction. Whatever object we examine, as long as the cause and conditions for the arising of its appearance are there, its nature is impermanence. Nothing that has taken birth may escape death. Furthermore, anything appearing in the external world is impermanent in nature. In particular, we should regard our own lives as impermanent. With the passing of every second, minute, hour, and day we move closer and closer to death—the ultimate illustration of our own impermanence. This realization should not serve to paralyze us with fear; on the contrary, it should give us the necessary motivation to practice the dharma with even more exertion and enthusiasm in preparation for our own death.

1.10 Worldly Activity Has No Benefit

Generally speaking, all worldly activity has no ultimate benefit; therefore it is considered the meaningless activity of samsara. Meaningless activity is defined by the struggle of sentient beings throughout the cyclic existence of samsara, as we repeat the same mundane activities over and over in the hope that this will bring us happiness and free us from suffering. However, these types of struggles actually just mire us deeper and deeper into the mud of samsaric existence, creating negative karmas that bind us to realms of pain, rather than free us into the bliss of enlightenment.

From an ultimate point of view, these meaningless, mundane activities leave us struggling and floundering like an elephant caught in quicksand; the more we struggle and fight, the deeper we sink. Although practicing desire and attachment towards near and dear ones such as our friends and family seems natural and would appear to bring us happiness, even these actions are meaningless ultimately. The happiness they do bring is only temporary and is, in fact, the source of our suffering, for attachments are truly negative behaviors that only create more negative karma, building more and more fences and walls around the prison of samsara that holds us locked into cyclic suffering.

The accumulation of material wealth throughout the entirety of this lifetime in the hopes that it will bring us happiness and satisfaction is meaningless from an ultimate point of view. The fact is that maintaining and protecting what we do have and struggling to acquire more only brings us more suffering and dissatisfaction; it's a bit like an old, toothless dog trying to chew a large, hard bone—meaningless! Try as he might, the dog will get no sustenance from that bone.

Any action performed by sentient beings out of ignorance is ultimately meaningless activity, like a blind man running headlong down a high mountain path; it is not likely he will reach his destination before falling to his death! Just so, when we operate from a position of ignorance, we will never reach our goal of liberation and enlightenment, but instead fall deeper and deeper into the realms of samsara. As long as our mind is infused with the six poisons, any relationship we have with others will only create harm because, from an ultimate point of view, we are like a deadly venomous snake whose bite will kill regardless of whether we intended any harm or not.

Our attachment to objects of desire, those things that please our six sense consciousnesses, is meaningless and harmful from an ultimate point of view. We are attracted to these things like a moth drawn to the luminosity of a candle's flame, and like that moth our wings will eventually be burnt as we fly too close and fall into a trap of hot wax.

In order to find liberation, we must detach ourselves from all of the meaningless activity of samsara and instead attach ourselves to activity that is positive from an ultimate point of view.

1.11 Examination of Life's Purpose

Examine closely which of your mundane activities are beneficial from the ultimate point of view. Examine closely your accumulation of material wealth, and how far you can carry it across the threshold of death. Examine closely why some sentient beings seem intent on causing us harm or wishing us ill when we are trying to help them out of compassion and kindness. Examine closely the inevitability that at the time of our own death we must undergo the experience and process of death and dying alone when, throughout our life, we are surrounded by billions of other human beings and countless other sentient beings. Examine closely the separation of the mind from the body, and why we have no control over death and the impermanence of our life. Examine closely just how far we can carry our name, fame, and power with us after death.

Closely and carefully examine all of these activities, their lack of essence, their lack of ultimate benefit, and ask, Why not meditate on my own mind? For the mind is the source of all activity, whether negative or positive.

1.12 Learning to Let Go

Generally speaking, dharma practitioners must practice renunciation by letting go of attachments to the daily mundane activities of everyday life. The reason behind the renunciation of mundane activity is not just that mundane activities have no essence, but that they are actually harmful in the sense that they strengthen the bonds that hold us tied to our experience of going around and around in cyclic existence.

We will not be able to liberate ourselves until we have cured our own karmic diseases; in order to cure ourselves of karmic disease we must let go by renouncing worldly actions of desire, aversion, and attachment. Instead, we must embrace meaningful and wholesome actions of body, speech, and mind. All ordinary beings are deceived by their experience of samsaric activities, believing in them, taking them as real, and becoming attached to them.

Furthermore, as long as our ego-clinging and the cravings it produces continue to increase in this samsaric existence, we will not be able to cut the root of samsara because we will be deceived by our own ego. When we let go of our notion of ego and its resulting desire, attachment, and aversion, the very roots of our sufferings in cyclic existence are cut through and liberation is attained. Ego is the source of all problems. As the author of all passions and aggressions it is the source of samsara, of good and bad, of black and white. We must learn to let go of the ego by meditating upon egolessness. Through practice, we can experience nondiscriminating wisdom, beyond the dualism of "I" and "other." We can experience the equanimity of the altruistic mind of the bodhisattva.

⚛ ————————————————————————————————————

As soon as we learn to let go of our own ego-clinging we begin to connect with the sacred dharma practice and its benefits, including the healing of our karmic disease in accordance with the buddhas and bodhisattvas.

1.13 What to Adopt or Discard

Relinquishing our desire for and attachment to the mundane phenomena of cyclic existence is extremely difficult as we travel the path towards liberation. Until we have reached the first bhumi on the bodhisattva path, when all actions are dharma practice, it is difficult to discard our tendency toward self-deception. Sentient beings trapped in samsara experience reality through the six sense consciousnesses, creating a false duality between subject and object, which leads to attachment and aversion toward certain experiences. We must discard these dualistic notions of subject and object in order to attain liberation.

As regular sentient beings, our time is consumed by ordinary mundane activity without any essence; we must discard this way of living our life and transform all activity into the bodhisattva path. To not make this transformation is to waste our time and energy on meaningless activity. The length of our lives is constantly shrinking, passing quickly like a car speeding toward its destination on a freeway, yet we continue to fill our days and nights with meaningless activity.

We must discard this mode of existence and replace it with the altruistic path of the bodhisattva, on which every action is a dharma practice for the limitless benefit of countless sentient beings. We've had since beginningless time to be involved with the pursuit of meaningless activity in cyclic existence; now it's time to discard this path in favor of larger pursuits and wholesome activities. We must contemplate and meditate on what to discard, and what to adopt—when we do, we are engaging in the practice of buddha dharma.

1.14 Cyclic Existence of Samsara

It is impossible to experience permanent happiness while our mind dwells in the physical state. From the moment of birth we embark on a search for happiness and meaning that lasts our entire lifetime, yet we fail to find either one. Until we have reached extremely high levels of attainment in our practice and achieved extraordinary powers of true mind over matter, the pain and suffering of body and mind will continue.

As long as we continue to have this experience of a precious human existence, there is always room and opportunity to improve towards ultimate happiness and bliss. Suffering does not end until the cause and effect of karma end.

The activities of sentient beings trapped in samsara are meaningless. As far as dharma practitioners are concerned, until we reach a level where we never regress, only progress, all activity is meaningless. Once we have taken refuge in the dharma and begun to practice, only virtuous actions have meaning—any nonvirtuous action is meaningless. Virtuous actions are those that have a positive result or benefit for ourselves or others; nonvirtuous actions are those that have no benefit or negative results, even if they are neutral. To give purpose to this human existence we must be of benefit to all sentient beings, including ourselves, through dharma activity. Otherwise, even a long life full of activity only results in even more lack of true meaning.

The best and most generous gift is the gift of dharma, if it is given with an altruistic attitude. Any other kind of gift is merely a temporary relief from the pain and suffering of samsara, while the gift of dharma provides us with another tool to uproot the very cause of suffering.

1.15 The Ultimate Purpose of Life

Life has no ultimate purpose unless we liberate ourselves from the suffering and pain of samsara through the practice of buddha dharma. Throughout our lives we might study and learn so many things, but these studies have no ultimate purpose if they do not serve to liberate us from the darkness of ignorance.

The time we spend with countless teachers, gurus, and lamas over the course of our lives has no ultimate purpose unless we receive the blessings and transmissions of their dharma lineage.

A lifetime spent mingling with a variety of yidam or deity practices has no ultimate purpose unless we receive genuine realization and mahasiddhi. Likewise, there is no ultimate purpose in a life spent practicing a variety of meditation techniques unless we develop one-pointed meditation.

When we spend our life struggling with negative afflictive emotions, it has no ultimate purpose unless we work to remove the root of these negativities through the practice of buddha dharma.

There is no ultimate purpose to a life spent going through the outer superficial motions and appearances of spiritual activity and practice with no genuine inner motivation driven by bodhichitta. In order for us to attain liberation, all of our outer spiritual activities and practice must be motivated by a sincere inner devotion to benefit all sentient beings through our limitless love and compassion.

1.16 Choose the Company of the Fortunate Ones

It is extremely important that we choose good company, particularly if we are on a spiritual path, because our body, speech, and mind are very easily influenced by people with whom we have close connection or frequent association. There are those unfortunate individuals who are extremely negative and have great amounts of defilements and obscurations. When we keep close company with such unfortunate ones, merely seeing them causes us to lose our faith and devotion in the dharma and obscures our connection to our own spiritual path. When we are friends with such unfortunate individuals, simply learning of their negative behavior and misdeeds pushes our own liberation further and further away. Mere memories of these friends cause negative afflicting emotions to arise, which results in the planting of even more seeds of cyclic existence. Any intimate contact with such unfortunate ones will cause us to lose our connection to the blessings and transmissions of our lama and yidams. Simply conversing with such unfortunate company will cause our attitude towards the Three Jewels to shift from positive to negative.

So associating with the unfortunate ones causes many obstacles in our path, and opens us to the blessings of demons and other negative spirits, which pushes self-liberation even further from our reach than before. Associating our own body, speech, and mind with the activity of the unfortunate ones causes our rebirth in one of the three lower realms.

1.17 A Proper Vessel Holds the Dharma Nectar

The vessel which becomes a carrier for the nectar of dharma consists of our body, speech, and mind. Within this vessel we must collect both merit and wisdom in order to benefit ourselves and others. To fill this vessel with merit and wisdom we must associate with and learn from spiritual friends who act from the altruistic mind of a bodhisattva. If we do the contrary, and we associate with those that operate from the confused, egocentric mind, our vessel becomes filled with poisonous negativities that dilute whatever small merit and wisdom we have.

Generating loving-kindness toward all sentient beings and performing acts of compassion will fill our vessel with merit and wisdom, while negative feelings and acts of selfishness and hatred will fill our vessel with the poison of negative karma, leading us back into the lower realms of cyclic existence. Until passion and aggression are removed from your heart and mind, they are like a burdensome rock of negativity that takes up so much room in your vessel that no room is left for anything else. When we remove the rock there is a spacious temple which can be filled with merit and wisdom.

The signs, or indications, that we have removed this rock of negativity and begun to fill that space with merit and wisdom are that we see positive thoughts, words, and deeds flowing from our body, speech, and mind toward all sentient beings.

It is also difficult to fill this vessel with merit and wisdom if we are holding on to negative emotions; it is like having our hands full of angry cobras and being unable to pick up or

1.18 Fruition of the Seed of Enlightenment

When we engage in virtuous actions, we realize they are beneficial not only for others, but also for ourselves. Our good deeds can earn the praise and appreciation of others, and the benefits of our work come back to us through others. When we are involved with virtuous works, people respect us and hold us in high esteem. And we know we must be doing something good, because we experience a wholesome, pleasant feeling about our life's work. We quickly begin to see the short-term benefits of our involvement in virtuous action as our bodies and minds become more peaceful in our daily lives.

This serenity in turn increases our longevity as our body and mind become more harmonized. Even after our death, we will be reincarnated in higher realms of existence as a result of our involvement with virtuous works during this life. Yet a higher rebirth is merely a short-term benefit, a temporary relief from the sufferings of samsara, for until we achieve liberation from samsara we remain trapped in the cycle of suffering, and "whatever goes up, must come down!"

Within the mundane world, when our evil deeds are common knowledge, no one sings their praises. If such deeds are remembered at all, it is in infamy. However, when a being lives with a mind of true bodhichitta and does great works of pure altruism, their deeds are remembered for centuries. Of such cases we have many examples within the Kagyu lineage alone: the historical Buddha, Guru Rinpoche, Milarepa, the Karmapas, and countless others. Yet it is also important to remember that virtuous action eventually leads us to the liberation of buddhahood; this is the ultimate long-term benefit of planting the seed of enlightenment of which we speak. Hence,

1.19 Life as Empty as a Dream

Nonvirtuous actions produce defilements and obscurations so thick and dark as to leave us blind, and no blind man can find the correct way to go when traveling. Like this proverbial blind man, we can become lost on our spiritual journey on the path to liberation. The obscurations created by nonvirtuous actions blind us by deluding our minds with desire and attachments to samsara, much like a man obsessed with beautiful women.

Nonvirtuous action renders our life's activities meaningless, making them no more significant than the projections on a movie screen, a nighttime dream, or a reflection in a mirror. These negative actions influence our mind in a way that we are transformed as if into small children on a playground, absorbed in games of make-believe and petty fights and quarrels. This deluded state of mind makes it nearly impossible for us to cut the ropes that bind us to samsara; we are like a fish caught on a hook, and once we've taken the bait, we cannot free ourselves, no matter how much we fight and struggle.

We must learn to not waste our lives in the pursuit of useless activities, and learn to instead follow a path of virtuous action that is productive for ourselves and others in both the short and long term.

1.20 Significance of Taking Vows

In order to liberate ourselves from samsara we can accumulate merit through the virtuous action of taking and keeping a variety of vows. However, the significance of the vows is such that we shouldn't keep them just because our teacher told us to or because the community we're in would frown upon us transgressing them; rather, we must keep them in our heart, we must keep them because we have voluntarily made a commitment to ourselves to follow these guidelines of moral conduct. If we take vows for any other reason, we are fooling ourselves. One of the roots of the doctrine of the buddha dharma is the practice of behavior that results in the fulfillment of moral ethics. The practice of taking and keeping vows of moral, ethical conduct has the same importance to our practice as soil does to the cultivation of crops—without taking and keeping vows of moral behavior, there is no way for our practice to grow. And without following the guidelines set forth by our vows, we become less able to differentiate moral from immoral behavior. Anywhere this ground of moral ethics exists, the crop of wisdom will naturally grow. In order to achieve rebirth in higher realms of existence, we must use moral and ethical conduct as a stairway there. Self-liberation is entirely dependent upon the self-discipline and self-control implicit in following moral conduct. Therefore, as dharma practitioners, it is essential that we understand the significance of keeping vows of moral conduct intact in order to attain liberation.

1.21 Consequences of Desire

Every ounce of physical and mental pain and suffering that we struggle with in this lifetime is completely and totally the karmic result of our desire from previous lifetimes. Any action we perform in this lifetime, whether physical or mental, determines which realm we will be reborn into in our next incarnation.

In fact, if we are born into one of the lower three realms in our next lifetime, we can trace this effect directly back to the negative desires and the actions they inspired in this lifetime. According to the teachings of the buddhas and bodhisattvas, our present quality of life is a direct consequence of our physical and mental actions in previous lifetimes, and any actions of body, speech, or mind in this lifetime plant the seeds that determine our realm of rebirth in future lives.

The reason that sentient beings experience a constant increase in negative afflictive emotions throughout this life, rather than relief from them, is that our daily lives are full of negative actions motivated by desire and attachment—a natural consequence of ego-clinging. Finally, any physical or mental action we perform that obscures the path of liberation is a consequence of negative karma.

1.22 Overcoming Negative Karma

Due to the influence of negative karma and a lack of clear understanding as to the purpose of life, we have a natural tendency towards engagement with samsaric activities and a forgetfulness of the impermanence of life and the certainty of our own death.

Due to the negative karma accumulated through our own ego-clinging—the attachment to the concepts of "self" and "other"—we treat other sentient beings with disrespect, not realizing that, ultimately, we have deceived ourselves and are operating from a position of ignorance and confusion.

Due to the influence of negative karma accumulated as a result of desire, we develop attachment to loved ones, indifference toward strangers, and aversion or even hatred toward enemies. We don't realize, of course, that ultimately we have deceived ourselves with this conditional love; we have failed to develop bodhichitta, which is unconditional love toward all living beings.

Due to the influence of our own negative karma, we fall into habits of selfishness, greed, and miserliness; ultimately we have deceived ourselves, for we have failed to practice contentment beyond conditions for the benefit of all sentient beings. Practicing contentment which transcends where we are, what we have, and who we are with is one of the most difficult practices for sentient beings still trapped in cyclic existence. Indeed, success in the practice of contentment is what draws a line between beginning and advanced practitioners.

Due to the influence of our own negative karma, we fall into laziness and procrastination and, ultimately, we deceive ourselves into failing to contemplate and meditate—the only practice that will free us from the bondage of this karma.

The only solution, the only thing that offers us a source of liberation from samsara, is to dig up the very root of negative karma by practicing the six perfections and increasing our merit and wisdom for the benefit of all sentient beings.

1.23 Investigating the Creator

What attitude is appropriate for practitioners on the path? We must realize that our entire world, including our happiness, desire, attachment, cravings, pain, and suffering—these things we deal with in everyday life—are none other than our own creation. They are the effect of our own past actions, our karma, and no one else can be blamed or held responsible for them. Once we realize this, we also recognize that our karma is no one's responsibility but our own—it is our own mess to clean up! This mess, this tangle of negative karma, is the source of all our suffering; we must find out how, when, and where it was created. We realize that some of this karmic mess was created previously and some is the result of present, ongoing actions. Karma has been created due to cause and effect, and that process depends on a creator. In our case, that creator is our very own mind. It is actually a confused state of mind that produces this cause and effect of karma. However, when a confused mind becomes transformed through purification, it begins to create positive karma through cause and effect. This is how we begin to remove obstacles to, and pass through the doorway to, liberation.

The process of birth, life, and death brings with it tremendous suffering, yet we accepted this suffering as part of the package at the moment we began this life at birth. If there were not birth and death, indeed there would be no suffering. Yet when we search this life for the "I" experiencing it, we cannot find it, no matter how we examine or investigate. No matter what method we use to try to locate a "self," we fail. If, for example, we are asked to point to "our self," where do we point? At our chest? For most of us here in the West, we tend to have the notion that our mind is located in our head, that it is our brain. Yet if we only had our brain, would we still be "us"? No matter how hard we look, we cannot identify one single part of ourselves that constitutes the "I" because each of these parts can be broken down into smaller and smaller parts.

Nevertheless, through our six senses we experience much pain and suffering in everyday life, so who is experiencing this suffering? This suffering is part of the package of rebirth that comes with the life we are experiencing. Cherishing, nurturing, and protecting this physical existence, this notion of "self," or "I," takes tremendous energy and causes us much suffering and pain. So as we cling to this ego-centered notion of existence, we cannot blame anyone else for our pain and suffering; it is our very own creation. We grasp at a dualistic notion of friend and enemy, and consequently we create love and hate in our mind. Encounters with enemies and separation from loved ones then cause us tremendous pain and grief. But this pain and grief are created by the very notion of friend and enemy in our mind.

Additionally, in the three lower realms—the hell realms, hungry ghost realm, and animal realm—individual beings experience unbearable pain and suffering. But even given these terrible states of existence, the Buddha stated that we cannot blame anybody else, for they are our very own creation through karma; we asked for it when we took the actions that caused these effects. Since it is our confusion, we must be the ones to clear it up.

1.24 Purification and Accumulation of Merit

While cultivating our attitude and behavior toward wholesome actions, it is advised that we make use of whatever wisdom we can find, without bias or discrimination. When we carry bias in our wisdom as practitioners we can fall into a sidetrack on our spiritual path. The idea of accumulating good karma through wholesome action is to purify our own afflictive emotions, and as we progress we should see our body, speech, and mind changing or transforming in positive ways. Our minds, for example, will become more calm and tranquil, such as when the turbulent rapids of a river become calm, allowing the mud and debris to settle so that the water clears and one can see the bottom. When our body and speech become calm and purified along with the mind, the result is that our outer actions become more kind, gentle, and compassionate, backed by an inner strength and confidence.

At this stage of purification through wholesome action we will begin to truly realize the impact of positive and negative actions, including long-term cause and effect. Naturally, we will accumulate merit and wisdom equally, just as a bird uses both wings to fly. In addition, we must reduce our negative emotions, in the same way that our body systems work to rid the body of poisonous toxins.

In order for our confidence and faith to grow, we must practice strict moral ethics, following a consistent and dependable code of conduct. When we plant the seed of morality and discipline, the tree of faith will grow naturally and beautifully.

1.25 Conquering Afflictive Emotion

In order to truly subdue the enemy of afflictive emotion, we must not practice sporadically, but with great diligence and consistency—to fully conquer afflictive emotions, our practice must be uninterrupted like the constant flow of a running river. The great practitioner will use the skillful means of method and wisdom to purify the negative karma he has accumulated since beginningless time. As serious practitioners we must accumulate both merit and wisdom together, side by side, if we are to achieve any significant work on eliminating our clinging to the concept of our own ego and obtain the ultimate realization of selflessness.

We and all sentient beings have been suffering from the sickness of karmic disease since beginningless time. Because of the depth to which this karmic disease keeps us mired in cyclic existence, our only cure is the medicine of dharma practice. Since we receive this precious medicine from our guru, we must always remain deeply devoted to that guru. The five poisons within us of our own karma are like a fiercely burning bonfire that can only be extinguished by the ocean of wisdom and compassion possessed by a bodhisattva. Finally, we must avoid further accumulation of negative karma that will carry us down into lower and lower realms of existence. To escape the negative momentum of our own karma we must rely upon the bodhisattva's path of liberation as if it were a stairway out of these lower realms.

1.26 The Antidote for Negative Karma

We must utilize the antidote available to us in the form of dharma practice in order to save ourselves from suffering from the poison of our own negative karma. The Three Jewels are the ultimate objects of veneration; therefore, we must make offerings to them and to the lamas, who are the nirmanakaya emanation of them, in order to benefit ourselves and others.

In order to cure ourselves of the afflictions of negative karma we must use the antidote of learning to let go of life's mundane activities, for there is nothing more important than letting go of our attachment to the mundane world.

Curing ourselves of negative karma includes using the antidote available through learning, contemplation, and meditation of the dharma. Using the antidote in this way to cure ourselves of negative karma also includes recognizing the buddha nature of our own mind through the guidance of our spiritual friends and gurus.

We must also use the antidote of engaging the altruistic mind of the bodhisattva to cut the very root of all selfishness. One of the signs that the dharma antidote has been applied properly and that the poison of negative karma has begun to dissipate is that we start to see the lama or guru as indistinguishable from the Buddha himself. This type of realization indicates that we are nearing the stage of the fulfillment of the ultimate wishes of liberation in order to limitlessly benefit all sentient beings.

1.27 Cause and Effect, Dependent Arising

According to the teachings of the sages, all things are dependent upon cause and effect. Therefore, two of the most important factors in our practice are faith and diligence, for if we do not plant these seeds, we will never see their fruits. Through faith and diligence, we don't simply remove negative emotions, but actually transform them into positive energy by using adverse conditions as a reminder of the impermanent nature of all phenomena.

When we recognize the infallible nature of karmic cause and effect, we learn to avoid negative actions of body, speech, and mind as if we were avoiding a poisonous plant or any other substance that would cause us harm. As we become more skillful in avoiding what is poisonous to us by stopping our accumulation of negative karma, our devotion increases to the point that our lama and spiritual friends are revealed to be no less than buddhas themselves. This occurs because as our karma improves and obscurations are removed we see things more clearly, just as a better camera lets us take a better picture.

In this way our certainty in the truth of the dharma and our confidence in our own practice increase to such a degree that our practice improves naturally and spontaneously. When these conditions are experienced by the fortunate dharma practitioner, they are an indication that negative karmic cause and effect are being transformed into positive karmic cause and effect.

2.1 Rarity of Human Birth

We need to recognize the rarity of our precious human birth and the opportunity for liberation it provides. When we come to this recognition we can use this human birth to its full potential. A human birth is considered to be so precious because it is the only realm of existence within which we can obtain liberation.

As an illustration of just how rare and precious a human birth is, think of this: although a human being seems quite common since we share the world with billions of other humans (and the world is getting more and more crowded), we may forget that the other five realms are filled with an infinite number of sentient beings as well. And while billions of humans may seem like a lot, it is actually quite a small number when compared to an infinite number. This is why birth in the human realm is considered not only precious but incredibly rare.

However, when we consider just how few of those billions of beings born into the human realm actually encounter, understand, and begin to practice the sacred dharma, and to fill their lives with meaningful actions of body, speech, and mind rather than the meaningless activity of ordinary mundane existence, it becomes even more clear what a rare opportunity we have as dharma practitioners. The number of humans that strive for not only their own liberation, but also for that of others, when compared to the number of humans simply wasting this rare and precious opportunity of human birth, shows that the precious human existence of a genuine dharma practitioner is truly as rare as seeing a star in the daytime.

In addition, it is even more rare and precious for the genuine dharma practitioner to then find a spiritual friend in a lama or guru who possesses true knowledge of wisdom and compassion, and rarer yet for that teacher to possess the oral transmissions of the teachings and blessings of a lineage. And finally, it is rarer still to find a dharma practitioner that is able to cut the root of delusion and move beyond the dualistic view of perceiver and perceived in order to liberate herself from cyclic existence.

2.2 Consequences of Procrastination

The teachings tell us that we should not waste this rare and precious gift of life as a human because of the infinite number of virtuous endeavors that we can accomplish with it. Yet what constitutes a precious life as opposed to a wasted life? A precious life is one that is spent accomplishing precious things for yourself and others. If nothing precious is gained for you or others through living this life, the life itself is not precious. We shouldn't allow our actions to become blocked by procrastination and distraction—our time in this life is short, and the end is always speeding towards us much more quickly than we can imagine.

If we waste our time in this life, our life loses meaning and ends with feelings of regret. Though we know that death is a certainty, this sense is worsened by the uncertainty of not knowing how soon death could occur; it could come for us at virtually any moment. What we experience in the life after death depends on the karma we carry with us, whether positive or negative. Through lack of positive karma or an abundance of negative karma we fall into one of the lower three realms. Within these three lower realms sentient beings experience such tremendous mental and physical suffering that following a path of practice toward liberation becomes impossible. Although sentient beings in the lower realms do have some notion or idea of how they came to be there and experience great regret for their previous life's nonvirtuous actions, they are so overwhelmed by their suffering and pain they cannot find the door of liberation—the opportunity to practice dharma is simply unavailable.

2.3 Looking Inward to Move Upward

We must look inward and locate the source of our mind's deception. Who is deceiving us? The answer is that our own mind is. In the very moment that we experience passion, aggression, or ignorance our mind's deception is taking place.

We must look inward to discover the relationship between our mind and body. Are they one and the same, or are they separate even while appearing to be one? We should come to realize the futility of our attachment to our physical form once our inward gaze has analyzed the constituents of which we are made. The four external elements of which we are composed are merely borrowed, and with our death are returned whence they came.

Our life seems to shine with the radiance and glory of a brightly lit butter lamp, but how long will it endure? Looking inward, we must see how much fuel remains and know when the lamp's light will fade and the dream of life will end.

With our inward looking we must also examine our accumulation of material wealth until we can rest in the certainty that these collections of physical objects are just another illusion in the dream of life, and that material wealth is of no real essence. Our drive to accumulate wealth impassions us to the point that we become like a World War II Kamikaze pilot whose mission was to defeat the enemy at the cost of his own life; the outcome of our mission to acquire more and more wealth becomes so focused that we are blinded to the fact that this behavior will lead us to our own end as well. We have to develop detachment from material things and the illusion of their importance. Think about it: after our death, even our most prized possession could be sold for a dollar at a garage sale.

By looking inward we must contemplate the ability of our spirituality to prepare us for our own death, for it is certain that the Lord of Death will come, and no one can escape his lasso. We should ask ourselves what practice we have undertaken day and night so that when Death comes with his rope, we can go without fear.

2.4 Separation of Mind and Body

As true dharma practitioners we must live in accordance with the ten wholesome actions and act in ways consistent with the principles of the buddha dharma so that we are completely free of regret and remorse at the time of our death. If we are true dharma practitioners, we spend so much time over the course of our lives associated with positive actions and practices to train our mind and to prepare ourselves for the moment of our own death that, when that moment comes, we do not experience fear or anxiety. Like an athlete that is well trained and about to enter competition, we are excited at the prospect of experiencing the transition out of this lifetime, for this transition brings the possibility of liberation and enlightenment.

As true dharma practitioners we must practice the perfection of generosity to such a degree that we become able to freely give up all that we have, without reservation or regret. When we do, we are able to remain unattached to this life at the moment of our death, allowing liberation to occur.

Finally, as true dharma practitioners we must diligently follow the three principles advocated by the Sage: moral conduct, meditation, and transcendent wisdom. If we follow these instructions throughout our entire lives, we will be so well prepared for our own death that we will experience no negative emotion when our mind separates from our body.

2.5 Dissolution of the Elements

Within the first bardo, or intermediate state, of the process of death we experience the dissolution of the connection between the mind and the physical body. These six bardos that appear to the minds of unenlightened beings are a mere appearance of superficial reality. However, these bardos do arise in the minds of confused beings and appear quite real to those still attached to samsara. The sages have said that, generally speaking, as long as we cling to the existence of samsara and nirvana, the existences of all sentient beings within the six bardos are included.

The first bardo is one of the most difficult times we experience as sentient beings. Due to the process of separation of mind from body, our mind becomes erratic in its perception of reality, shifting alternately between experiences of luminous clarity and terrifying states of darkness and confusion. These unusual experiences that result from erratic states of mind are the signs and symptoms of the impending separation of mind and body.

During the process of death, the elements that comprise our physical existence become imbalanced and begin to separate from each other. As a dying being, our own earth element dissolves into the external universal earth element and becomes so heavy as it descends that it becomes impossible for us to sit up or hold our position without assistance. Our water element dissolves into the external water element, leaving our limbs and organs dry and shrunken; even the color of our flesh fades, giving us the appearance of extreme dehydration. Furthermore, our air element dissolves, and this can be observed in the quality of our breath and our pulse as we are dying. If our breathing becomes shallow, labored, short or rapid, or even stops outright, and if the pulse becomes weak or ceases altogether, these are all signs of the dissolution of the air element.

In addition, the fire element fades from our extremities into the heart chakra, leaving our limbs cold and feeling dead. However, there should be some amount of life left in the form of heat around the area of the heart, because we are not yet completely dead. The extremely advanced practitioner will continue to maintain this heat around the heart chakra while maintaining the physical meditation posture even after breathing and heartbeat have ceased, and this meditative samadhi can be maintained for up to a week. It is recommended that such a practitioner not be disturbed until he is no longer able to maintain the seated meditation position. We can see how close to death he or she is by pinching a small amount of skin and observing how quickly it returns to its original shape.

Each of these elements is borrowed from the universe at the moment of our conception in our mother's womb. At the completion of the process of separation between mind and body during the process of death, these elements are returned to the universe. During this process, a darkness closes in as we begin to lose the ability to perceive through the five ordinary senses. As the external senses shut down, it's like the sun setting on this lifetime, and the day of this life transforms into a moonless night. At this time our internal sense consciousness also begins to experience a feeling of being trapped. As the light fades from the outside world, the mind races but is caught like a bee in a jar—it buzzes around desperately, but no matter how much or how fast it flies, it cannot escape because the lid is closed. Each of the five external sense consciousnesses, or skandhas, disconnects and is no longer able to function and provide perception of the external world. The eye consciousness ceases to provide perception of form, the ear consciousness ceases to provide perception of sound, and so on. As each of these five skandhas ceases to function, they merge with the sixth, the mind consciousness.

At this point in the death process, we will no longer respond to external stimuli, yet we are not truly dead. The mind consciousness has reached the border between life and death. In buddha dharma terms, we have entered the ultimate mandala. At the threshold of this borderline between life and death, upon entering the ultimate mandala, we will have either positive, welcoming experiences or negative, terrifying experiences. Our experience at this moment is entirely dependent upon our karma: if we have led a life focused on spiritual development, love, kindness, and compassion, our mind will experience the welcoming visions of paradise. But if our life was filled with anger, hatred, and aggression, our experience will be one of looking into a terrifying realm inhabited by deadly demons and monsters.

When we are initially conceived in the womb of our mother, we inherit two drops, or bindhu, from our parents. The white drop, received from the father, is located at the crown chakra of a living being. The red drop, received from the mother, is located at the root chakra. At the time of death, however, as we enter the ultimate mandala, these two bindhu move towards each other to alaya, or fundamental consciousness, at the heart chakra.

When the two drops meet with the fundamental consciousness, the experience of dying beings differs. For some, the experience is like an earth-shattering explosion and the mind is finally and completely separated from the body. For others, the experience of separation is one of openness, luminosity, and clarity, like emerging into a glimmering cloudless sky. Whichever experience occurs, we can say that at this point the process of death is complete and we have entered the second bardo. This intermediate state between our death and our next rebirth, also called the sidpa bardo, is known as the bardo of becoming.

2.6 Mind beyond Death

We must learn that ultimate truth is beyond death. We must learn that our own intrinsic wisdom is beyond death. We must learn that the luminosity of dharmakaya is beyond death. We must learn that the undeceivable infallibility of karmic cause and effect is beyond death.

We must learn that space is beyond the extremes of hope, fear, doubt, and expectation; rather, it is limitless in its unobstructed possibility and therefore beyond death. We must learn to let go of our own ego-clinging, and realize the selflessness that is beyond death.

If we have attained these ultimate realizations, we can never be captured by the Lord of Death when he casts his net —we will continually slip through because we, too, will have moved beyond death.

2.7 Love without Expectation

Worldly pleasures such as name, fame, power, and wealth are inseparable from impermanence, and thus as true dharma students we should remain unattached and practice renunciation of those worldly pleasures and comforts.

These worldly dharmas can be used for the benefit of our dharma practice and all sentient beings, but only if we remain unattached to them. Your name and fame are impermanent, and although they can be as magnificent as the thunder and lightning of the most powerful storm, they quickly dissipate into the quiet of gentler weather.

Your wealth is also impermanent, for although it can be as great as the thickest and heaviest clouds that cover the four quarters of the sky, we should not become attached to wealth because it can be scattered as quickly as the wind scatters the clouds, leaving us with a clear sky.

It is also important to realize that these worldly dharmas of wealth and fame can be quite beneficial to us as dharma students if we use them for the benefit of our dharma practice as well as for the benefit of all sentient beings. These worldly dharmas actually pose no problem whatsoever as long as we remain unattached to them and maintain the understanding of their impermanence. These worldly dharmas will surely be of no use at the time of death: when the mind separates from the body, it leaves all worldly dharmas behind.

In our mundane existence, we develop love, affection, and even great attachment for many near and dear ones over the course of our lives. This does not necessarily create problems for us as true practitioners as long as we cultivate the understanding that these relationships we form are impermanent and we don't allow our attachment to them to become obstacles to our dharma practice. In fact, for most of us these relationships actually provide us a reference point from which we learn to cultivate our love for all sentient beings without exception and free of conditions.

We also tend to develop affection towards our home and homeland, and this also is not necessarily negative as long as we continue to extend our understanding of the impermanence of our life in this home, and do not allow this affection to become an obstacle to our practice due to attachment and habitual behavior. The comfort and stability provided by a secure home can actually benefit our practice by allowing us more time and energy to practice the dharma and work to benefit others, but only if we can remain unattached to this home, which we should see simply as a tool to be used for the ultimate good.

Finally, as genuine dharma students we should neither develop attachment to pleasure and comfort nor aversion to pain and suffering, for they are like a dream, or like a reflection in a mirror—impermanent and empty of inherent existence.

2.8 Use the Worldly Dharmas

The genuine practitioner must focus entirely on the path of liberation, committing all resources to the goal of enlightenment rather than devoting excessive energy to the eight worldly dharmas, such as the obsessive accumulation of material wealth. Of course, should material wealth arise during the course of the practitioner's spiritual efforts, this is not necessarily an obstacle so long as this wealth is not the focus or the intended result of those spiritual efforts. In fact, if the practitioner has proper motivation, material wealth can actually be used to help alleviate suffering and other obstacles on the path.

Nor should a practitioner devote his life's energy to gaining many fans and followers, for whatever fame he gains will not help on his path to enlightenment. While it would be beneficial to have a great number of dharma devotees of great quality following a teacher of great quality, we can clearly see that the quality of the practitioner is far more important than the quantity of practitioners. So rather than focusing energy on accumulating the worldly dharmas of name and fame, the genuine practitioner will focus his efforts on the altruistic path of the bodhisattva. If through his effort to benefit all sentient beings the practitioner gains fame or notoriety spontaneously, as a mere side effect of his spiritual efforts, this does not pose an obstacle to his dharma path because it is not the intended result or main focus of his practice.

As genuine practitioners we selflessly focus our energy and efforts on the benefit of others. When we carry the realization that there are infinite numbers of beings suffering in samsara, how important is a single individual (us) when compared to all of these others? When we look at the situation this way, it becomes obvious that as true practitioners we must dedicate ourselves, first and foremost, to the liberation of all sentient beings. However, should any relief from our own suffering arise, whether mundane, material comforts, or even attainments of great realization, this does not pose an obstacle to our dharma path so long as they are not the focus or hoped-for result of our practice. The alleviation of the suffering of others is always put before our own, for there is no true separation between ourselves and others, and to ease their suffering is to ease our own.

2.9 Obstacles to Practice

Common practitioners can make mistakes in their practice which become obstacles in their path. One major mistake is that we can become egocentric or arrogant, feeling or thinking we are more important or powerful than others. This inflated view of ourselves creates a serious obstacle to our dharma practice. After all, a key recognition of the bodhisattva path is to see that we are not separate from other sentient beings, and should therefore share a sense of equality with them.

A second major mistake that becomes an obstacle to our practice is to become distracted by the mundane activities of everyday life; from the bodhisattva point of view these mundane activities have no essence and so are a complete waste of our time and life.

A third major mistake is in thinking that if we can exercise effort and diligence in our mundane endeavors, they will eventually provide us with happiness and fulfillment—a release from our sufferings. Whatever relief we gain from these mundane endeavors, however, is always temporary and impermanent, and actually becomes an obstacle to liberation. Instead, we must learn to exercise this kind of diligence in our practice of the bodhisattva path.

Yet a fourth major mistake is in our choice of a guru. Many find it easy to admire someone who is rich, powerful, or famous; yet these attributes are all part and parcel of the same cycle of suffering we are trying to escape. Instead, we must choose whom to look up to as an example for living based on the path they have traveled out of this cycle of suffering and into liberation. We must choose a buddha. If we are truly yogis and yoginis then make no mistake—we have transformed the five poisons into wisdom and developed our bodhichitta toward all sentient beings.

As practitioners we can create a major obstacle in our practice and obscure our mind by pretending to be a great meditator or holding the wrong view that we are a higher-level meditator. This act of self-deception on our part can be an obstacle. We must eliminate as many mistakes in our practice as possible so that we may lessen the obstacles we encounter. In doing so, our perseverance will increase and we will continue swiftly toward the door of liberation.

2.10 Avoid Sidetracks

As practitioners we will face many obstacles and sidetracks on our path to liberation, and these will provide us with many challenges along the way. We shouldn't allow our practice to become interrupted due to these obstacles and sidetracks, such as the appearance and disappearance of the many friends we will have over the course of our lives.

We also shouldn't allow our practice to become interrupted by a change in the availability or quality of food and shelter. And we shouldn't allow our practice to become interrupted by the obstacles and sidetracks presented by the many distractions of mind that are readily available in the mundane world of our external environment. We shouldn't allow our practice to be interrupted by obstacles and sidetracks that arise due to the desire and attachment we feel for loved ones, or our aversion to enemies, or our indifference towards others. Finally, we should not allow our practice to become interrupted by our desire to accumulate wealth, or by our attachment to our material possessions. Only an advanced practitioner, motivated by deep bodhichitta, can get through these obstacles and avoid these sidetracks to reach their goal of liberation from samsara.

2.11 Obstacles as Opportunities

When you do finally find a genuine guru, the first thing you should do is enlist his or her help to disperse any doubts that cloud your faith and devotion towards your practice. When you encounter obstacles to your dharma practice, rather than complaining and allowing them to cause you to backslide, you should instead view those obstacles and challenges as opportunities, and use them to fuel your practice. When you receive the sacred lineage transmission, you must not allow yourself to simply rest in contentment and complacency; rather, you must increase your practice in accordance with the instructions of that transmission, while at the same time decreasing your involvement with and attachment to mundane concerns and activities in order to free more of your mind, time, and energy so that they may instead be committed to dharma practice. When you experience great enthusiasm and diligence while on the path of your daily practice, you must remember that your road will not always be smooth and easily traveled; instead you should expect the ups and downs, bumps, and even roadblocks that form the inevitable obstacles, and view them as opportunities to persevere, adapt, and overcome.

When you have experiences of great understanding and realization as a result of your dharma practice, you must remember that the outcomes from these experiences can actually be negative if you allow yourself to become attached to them or become complacent, arrogant, or prideful. These experiences should never be seen as a goal that provides the driving reason behind your practice: when they are, you succumb to the forces of hope and fear that only create more obstacles to your

2.12 Accumulation of Wealth

When we accumulate wealth for our own benefit alone, it brings only temporary relief from the sufferings of this existence. However, if our purpose in collecting material things is that we may be able to help others when they are in need by practicing generosity through the sharing of our wealth, then our actions can produce an ultimate benefit that transcends relative existence.

Imagine a king born into the wealthiest of families. Without generosity all his wealth and riches are completely pointless, for we all must leave every single one of our material possessions behind when we die, regardless of our station in life. The ultimate benefit from any action is liberation from samsara. Throughout our lives, from the moment of our birth to the moment of our death, any action or effect of an action that does not move us or sentient beings toward that end is pointless.

2.13 Obscuration of Ego

One of the greatest obstacles we can face as practitioners is to pretend we know the genuine dharma when, in truth, we have no more understanding of the dharma than any ordinary being. In fact, those that believe they are great practitioners often possess even less attainment and realization than other ordinary beings. For instance, there are those practitioners who claim to have entered into the commitments of the doctrine of the buddha dharma, but who continue to commit negative actions in direct contradiction to the sacred dharma, and therefore continue to accrue negative karma. This scenario is even worse than ordinary beings committing these same misdeeds, for an ordinary being has violated no sacred commitments.

There are some Mahayana and Vajrayana practitioners so obscured by their pride and ego that they think they are superior to others. However, in actuality they are even more confused than those ordinary beings that hate the dharma. There are also those that claim to be dharma practitioners who are less focused on their dharma practice than they are on mundane activities—to the point that they are more involved with mundane activities than ordinary beings that practice no dharma at all.

There are even those so enveloped in obscurations and defilements that, rather than being proponents of the doctrine and their lineage, are actually a disgrace to the dharma and destroyers of the Sage's doctrine.

2.14 Signs of Ripening

There are many signs which serve as indications that a dharma student has begun to ripen. These indications are quite complicated to interpret, however, for between inner and outer indications there are actually four possible permutations that can exist in any given student:

1. the outer appearance of ripening but inner lack thereof;
2. an actual inner ripening with no outer appearance thereof;
3. signs of ripening both inside and outside; and
4. lack of ripening both inside and outside.

Just as with fruit, a student's ripening is a matter of timing. Pulling fruit from a tree that has yet to ripen is simply a waste of what would have eventually been a good food but is currently unpleasant. A student who has yet to ripen may encounter the teachings, but if the timing is not right, they will express no interest in dharma practice. A student not yet ripened is like a bucket that has been placed upside down; with proper placement the bucket could be used to hold and carry water, but currently it is ineffective. Just so, the unripened dharma student cannot understand or, at worst, cannot even hear the teachings of the dharma when they are given. They are a vessel that cannot hold or carry the nectar of dharma because it is currently upside down!

Another metaphor for the unripened student is that he is like a vessel which, although it is right side up, has a hole in the bottom and therefore cannot hold water. For this student, the practices done or teachings heard are never retained. A student unready to ripen also has many doubts and expectations about their dharma practice—they have become a vessel that holds poisons of doubt along with the water that make the water unsafe for anyone to drink.

A dharma student not ready to ripen can also be like a bucket that has no room for water because it is filled with the sand of pride and arrogance. This student's ego, swollen with the books she has read and the words she knows, takes up so much space that there is no room left for the true realizations of the dharma.

Finally, a student is clearly unready to ripen when he has difficulties staying on track and maintaining a consistent dharma practice. He continually strays from the dharma path into the jungle of samsara, wandering in circles trying to find his way back to the path. He finds his way back, only to wander off again and again.

3.1 Stepping onto the Intermediate Path

In the mundane world we focus so much of our time and energies on planning for our future benefit in terms of material comfort, such as making elaborate plans for business development in the hopes of future profit, that we are sowing the seeds of material gain in hopes of a future harvest of mundane benefit. As we step onto the intermediate path, however, we must begin to see that these plans only lead us back into samsara. In making such an adjustment in outlook, we can begin to sow the seeds of virtuous action that will lead us to a harvest of liberation and bliss.

Generally speaking, human beings compete for finite resources in a world where any gain that one being makes signifies that much less for everyone else. We constantly strive to gain more for ourselves—a bigger, better slice of the pie, so to speak. But as with a pie there is only so much to go around, and if one has a larger piece, others must have a smaller one. However, as we begin to walk the intermediate level of the dharma path we become more concerned with the benefit of others and our natural, ingrained competitive logic is reversed: we begin to be less concerned with ourselves and to desire more and better for others.

Another natural tendency of sentient beings is to love and cherish their near and dear ones, that is their own family and friends; however, as we step onto the intermediate level of the path, this discriminating love is overwhelmed as our love begins to expand and extend to all sentient beings equally and indiscriminately. As a matter of fact, as we enter the intermediate level of our practice, we move beyond love and hatred of friends and enemies and come to rest in equanimity, an impartial love for all beings that goes beyond attachments or aversions.

So at this intermediate level of practice we must practice the expansion of love and compassion, as well as the accumulation of merit and wisdom, rather than pursue the accumulation of illusory material wealth like a bee that toils its entire life collecting pollen to make just enough honey for the temporary happiness of a passing bear, who eats a little and then moves on!

As we move on through this life, to death, and into the next life, these material things we have collected and left behind no longer bring us any benefit, but our compassion, merit, and wisdom will always remain with us. As dharma practitioners at the intermediate level, our greatest enemies and greatest obstacles are procrastination and a scattered, unfocused mind. When these obstacles are overcome we will have conquered the only enemy that keeps us from liberation.

3.2 Enslaved by Material Wealth

We should be aware of the many sidetracks that become available when we begin to follow the dharma. We must aim high and remain focused on the larger goal of ultimately benefiting ourselves and others, rather than get distracted by the many meaningless small projects and interests of mundane existence. We must not fall into the sidetracks of the worldly dharmas, such as accumulation of wealth and fame, for in the end these will show no ultimate benefit for us or other sentient beings.

We must not become sidetracked by greed or miserliness, for while the practice of generosity extends to both oneself and others, it is based solely on what resources we have available to us at a given time. If you encounter a legitimate need for help and you do not have the resources within your means to give that help, you should maintain the pure intention of giving assistance if you ever become able. If you hold this intention as well as offer the heartfelt aspiration prayers that you will one day have that ability to help, then in this instance you have furthered your practice of the perfection of generosity.

We must avoid the sidetrack that awaits us when we become enslaved by our focus on the accumulation and hoarding of material wealth, for then these resources are never used for the enjoyment or benefit of oneself or others.

So rather than placing our faith and confidence in the worldly dharmas and falling into sidetracks such as taking refuge in our accumulated material wealth, we must instead devote our faith and confidence to the genuine buddha dharma, for without that faith and confidence, although we may see some benefits from our practice, we will never receive the ultimate blessings and transmissions that come with the only true refuge, which is our refuge in the Three Jewels.

3.3 Self and Selflessness

As genuine Mahayana practitioners we combine bodhichitta and aspiration prayers to form our daily practice. If either one of these ingredients is lacking, we are like a one-winged bird trying to fly. In order to benefit limitless sentient beings through bodhichitta, the great compassion, we must completely let go of our own selfishness and fully embrace self-sacrifice. Once we have set foot upon the Mahayana path, the degree to which we can claim to be a true Mahayana practitioner is directly proportional to the degree to which we are capable of completely abandoning the idea of the self and embracing self-sacrifice in order to benefit others.

Once our confused notion of self has ceased and our every action forms part of our Mahayana practice to benefit all sentient beings, without exception, then buddhahood is attained.

We will not attain realization by simply hiding from the rest of society, hidden in seclusive retreat. Our mind itself must change so that self-cherishing is released and self-sacrifice is embraced. Perfect realization cannot be attained until the Mahayana practitioner's mind is completely purified of the three poisons of passion, aggression, and ignorance.

Finally, we must make aspiration prayers, powered by faith and devotion, that we may be showered by a rain of blessings that bathes us in the fruition of the transmissions of the buddha dharma.

3.4 The Virtue of Patience

It is essential for dharma practitioners to develop the virtue of patience in order to liberate ourselves and others. We must practice patience by learning not to attach our own emotional reactions to others' words of praise or criticism, and instead see those words for what they are: mere sounds that are empty of any true essence, like an echo rolling through a valley.

In order to plant the seed of patience we must practice by not allowing the passions and aggressions of others to affect our own mind's emotional state. We can plant the virtuous seed of patience by examining our own minds and actions to see that they are never in contradiction with the doctrines of the buddha dharma. In order to plant the virtuous seed of patience we must also develop the altruistic mind of bodhichitta by practicing the perfection of generosity. Rather than selfishly working for the accumulation of material wealth for ourselves, we must share our wealth with others that are in need, without reservation. This will bring us to the highest level of the perfection of patience.

As dharma practitioners, to perfect our patience we must fully embrace and fully experience all of our obstacles and all our pain and suffering; in essence, all our own karma. We must see this karma for what it is, fully accept it, and then use it as fuel for our own practice, as an opportunity to transform ourselves.

Finally to perfect our patience we must continually work to improve our faith and devotion until we have become bodhisattvas able to work tirelessly for the limitless benefit of all sentient beings.

3.5 Activity of Ultimate Benefit

It is extremely important for a dharma practitioner to know which activities bring us benefit or harm from an ultimate perspective. According to the dharma, this human life we currently experience is actually extremely short. We typically live less than a single century, yet we have countless lives still ahead of us—more cycles than we can imagine of being born, living, and dying. We must use this realization of just how short this life is to fuel our dharma practice so that we can ultimately benefit ourselves and others. For example, if we are selfish, greedy, and miserly in this lifetime, we are sure to experience both material and spiritual poverty in this lifetime as well as throughout our future lives. However, if we are more concerned with engaging in activities of ultimate benefit, such as practicing the first paramita of the six perfections, working to constantly improve our practice of generosity towards others, we ensure that at both a material and spiritual level we will continue to experience richness and plenty throughout our future lives.

In order to upgrade ourselves to higher and higher levels of existence, we must continue to engage ourselves in activities of ultimate benefit by practicing the second paramita—the perfection of moral discipline. Moral discipline is like a stairway that allows us to climb ever upwards into higher levels of existence, and without it there is absolutely no other mechanism for us to move upwards toward buddhahood.

We must then further our engagement in activities of ultimate benefit by moving into the third paramita—the perfection of patience. When we practice the perfection of patience it is as if we are standing in the middle of a chaotic battlefield, but as the war rages on around us we are completely protected by the impenetrable armor of our perfect patience.

The fourth paramita is the perfection of diligence, or perseverance. As we practice diligence we experience a great accumulation of wisdom. The perfection of diligence is like learning a new language—we begin with a word at a time until we are able to put together sentences and eventually compose whole paragraphs and have conversations.

Our experience with activities of ultimate benefit deepens even further as we begin to practice the fifth paramita—the perfection of meditation. Our meditation, when perfected, should be one-pointed to such a degree that we experience no movements or shifts in our mind stream whatsoever, like a candle flame burning brightly, unwavering, that will not even flicker in a passing breeze.

Finally, in order to engage in activities of ultimate benefit and fulfill all wishes of ourselves and others, we must practice the sixth paramita—the perfection of wisdom. When our wisdom is perfected we become like the sun and the moon, lighting the way for all without any effort or exertion.

3.6 Doorway to Liberation

To find the doorway to liberation, we must fully dedicate our body, speech, and mind to wholesome actions. To do this, we must completely rid ourselves of laziness and procrastination. In addition, we need to dedicate all the material resources at our disposal to finding the door to liberation.

Since we have dedicated our body, speech, and mind to the attainment of buddhahood, there should be no question that our every possession is also dedicated to that same end. In order to purify ourselves—completely cleanse our body, speech, and mind of negative karma—we should use the tools available to us through the buddha dharma. These numerous techniques include feeling regret or remorse for our transgressions, confession of our failures, and the renewal of our vows, again and again, in order to maintain the pure outlook and conduct (including rules and regulations) of bodhisattvas.

We must develop the strength to travel the path of a bodhisattva with diligence and consistency, avoiding the failures of sidetracks and backward steps. Following the path of the bodhisattva means taking the path of purification of our body, speech, and mind, and taking this journey toward liberation also means accumulating both merit and wisdom. Accumulating both merit and wisdom is a lot like needing two legs to walk properly; a man with one leg may still make some progress forward, but the advantage of walking on two legs is clear! Another metaphor we can use is that of a bird in flight. Developing both merit and wisdom together as a pair is as important as a bird needing both wings to fly; with only one wing the bird would never get into the sky.

Building an entire house from the ground up takes much

skill and effort, but anyone can burn it down quite easily. Similarly, it requires much more merit and wisdom to engage in wholesome or virtuous endeavors than it does to commit negative actions. When we are following the path of the bodhisattva we must remember three important aspects of our practice:

- At the onset, we must take refuge and generate bodhichitta toward all sentient beings.
- In the middle and throughout the practice, we must always follow the guidelines of the bodhisattvas, and never stray from this code of conduct (rules and regulations).
- In the end, we must dedicate the merit of our practice to the benefit and complete liberation of all sentient beings.

Developing the dual virtues of merit and wisdom facilitates our ability to maintain these three aspects of our practice while on our path toward liberation. Maintaining the vows and conduct (activities) of a bodhisattva brings us closer and closer to the door of liberation every day.

3.7 Cutting the Bonds of Delusion

As practitioners of the sacred dharma we are required to learn to cut the bonds of our own afflictive emotions. Cutting through these afflictive emotions includes severing our attachment to and desire for the objects of our six senses, for liberation comes only by digging up the very root of cyclic existence. We dig up these roots of samsara by ceasing all harmful and meaningless activities in order to cut the bonds of our kleshas and stay on the right path towards buddhahood.

We can cut through the bonds of our own delusion by recognizing that when we develop desire and attachment for objects of our senses, we are fooled into chasing an illusion that only keeps us trapped in cyclic existence. We must cut the bonds of our kleshas by letting go of our attachment to our own ego, embodied by our desire for name, fame, and respect—all part of the worldly dharmas of mundane existence.

We must cut through our deluded notions of friends and enemies, for those designations are dualistic and completely conditional; they are merely dependently-arisen phenomena, mental reflections of our own negative emotions. Instead, we must follow the path of the bodhisattva and embrace the idea of equanimity, or unconditional love and compassion towards all sentient beings.

When we cut through the bonds of our kleshas, we begin to dig up the very root of our delusions, the cause of all pain and suffering in samsaric existence, and attain the bliss of realization of the ultimate view.

3.8 The Application of Dharma

We must have a sincere interest in the dharma. Having this sincere interest, we should study and contemplate the teachings with diligence. Without such a genuine interest in the dharma, we will not truly hear it, even if we attend hundreds and hundreds of teachings. We should rejoice in what we have already learned, no matter how little, and celebrate the practices in which we are currently involved. We shouldn't become discouraged on the path to liberation. Unless we plant the seeds of liberation, our suffering in the cyclic existence of samsara will continue forever. We plant this dharma seed of enlightenment in the soil of our own mind, and our genuine interest is what makes the soil rich and fertile so that the fruits of liberation may one day blossom. However, we must continually nurture this seed with our daily dharma practice. Though in general samsara has no end for most sentient beings, the virtuous action of dharma can provide our minds with what is necessary to break out of this perpetual cycle—this is liberation.

3.9 Dedication without Regret

When we dedicate our body, speech, and mind to dharma practice and bodhisattva activities, even at the cost of our very lives, we should make this sacrifice without the slightest regret or hesitation. While following the path of the bodhisattva, even if the whole world treats us with cruelty and disrespect because of our practice, even if we are looked upon with absolute derision and ridicule because of our view and our path, we should not hesitate or regret our commitment, but rather use such resistance to fuel our confidence and the energy of our practice. We should give up our very homelands without regret, as this journey of liberation requires the practice of detachment.

Even if the practice of bodhichitta should leave our stomachs grumbling with hunger and our mouths parched with thirst, still we should have no regret in our choice to follow the bodhisattva path for the benefit of all sentient beings. For the purpose of purification, we must not regret the cleansing of negative action and negative karma, even though many of us are profoundly attached to our bad habits and wrong views. When we wash our clothes, we don't miss the dirt! Likewise, when we purify our mind, we must detach from all that is nonvirtuous and dedicate our lives to the virtuous, without regret or hesitation.

3.10 Action without Bias

Generally speaking, sentient beings have an attachment or preference for their own "nest," or home, and their own country or nation. However, as part of our dharma practice we must develop an equanimity towards all nests, and all nations, with no bias or discrimination. We must not fall into the two extremes of eternalism or nihilism, but instead go beyond them. When we do transcend these two extremes, we are led into liberation.

3.11 Importance of Perfect Motivation

Our motivation is extremely important when we wish to follow in the steps of buddhas and bodhisattvas. We must be motivated by the pure altruistic mind of the bodhisattva to practice the dharma for the benefit of all sentient beings. If the motivation behind our dharma practice is impure, then we will not succeed in removing the hangman's noose of samsara from around our neck. A pure motivation frees us from the gallows by making our practice more productive. It produces more positive results in our dharma practice and prevents us from falling into the tangle of samsara's activities. For instance, if our motivation is impure, we might fall into dysfunctional relationships with neither a way to solve the problems nor a way out of the relationship itself. Right motivation toward buddha dharma enables us to make sound decisions regarding our life's activities—like a developed instinct about what we should and should not eat based on what is nutritious as opposed to poisonous.

Pure motivation toward bodhichitta increases the strength of our realization so that we can better distinguish between reality and illusion. Pure motivation deepens our realization and understanding to the point that we can prevent the deceptions inherent in the fabric of the mundane world. Without this clear view and understanding of reality, we are easily deceived, even by those we feel we love and trust.

Without the pure motivation of bodhichitta in our practice, we will not be able to practice the middle path of impartiality and equanimity in the development of our loving-kindness and compassion toward all sentient beings; instead we'll fall into the extremes of enemies and friends, obsessed love and

3.12 Decrease to Increase

In order to increase our wisdom and compassion, we must first increase our helpful actions and decrease or eliminate our harmful ones. At the same time, we must constantly improve our mindfulness and awareness.

Additionally, if we are to liberate ourselves from samsara, we must increase both our patience and the enthusiastic determination we carry into our dharma practice. When we cultivate this attitude of patience combined with enthusiastic effort, it is possible to cut the root of cyclic existence. Armed with this attitude, we can overcome any obstacles that appear on our dharma path toward enlightenment. We must also cultivate an understanding that the life we are presently living is extremely short, especially in contrast to the combined length of all our potential future lives stretching into the infinite future. When we feel confidence in this realization, we are able to dedicate every action to enlightenment, rather than to the worldly dharmas that bring us only temporary relief in this lifetime alone. With this realization, our understanding of the goal of liberation will have more depth and clarity, and we'll spontaneously develop more skill in dealing with any situation that arises.

Finally, at this level of our development we are able to recognize and address our own faults and stop focusing on the shortcomings of others.

3.13 Cultivating Wisdom

In order to attain a genuine understanding of the buddha dharma, we must develop our innate wisdom. If we do not yet seem to possess it, we must begin to cultivate it. We can cultivate our wisdom by learning, training, and meditating. To become learned in skillful means we must study under the guidance of learned and skillful masters. Cultivating our own wisdom takes tremendous time and patience, and we must never become complacent in our satisfaction with the knowledge and wisdom we have gained so far. We must not be satisfied until we have achieved liberation.

We must cultivate our wisdom so that, through our wisdom eye, we can see clearly and differentiate right from wrong among the chaos and confusion of the mundane world. This insight enables us to act in a virtuous and wholesome manner so that we may eventually attain liberation. The ultimate achievement for any human being is the complete fulfillment of both our own wishes and the wishes of other sentient beings. This is only attainable through the cultivation of our own wisdom.

We must cultivate our own wisdom so that we may come to see our spiritual friends, our gurus, for the genuine spiritual masters they are. This will endow us with the faith and the confidence required to truly rely upon our teachers so that we may benefit from our practice exactly as our masters have benefited from theirs.

We cultivate our wisdom by collecting as much wisdom as we can from as many different sources as we can; we don't discriminate against any of the infinite number of sources available. Although our accumulation may begin as a mere trickle, one drop at a time, it slowly grows into a stream which eventually swells into a river. This flowing river, over time, fills the unfathomable breadth and depth of an ocean—an ocean of infinite wisdom. Once we have obtained this ocean of infinite wisdom, an unshakable certainty and confidence in our practice arises in our mind, and this opens up many doorways so that we may benefit countless sentient beings on their path towards enlightenment.

3.14 To Conquer the Maras

As practitioners of the genuine dharma, we must come to rely upon the Three Jewels completely and without reservation. This foundation allows us to begin renunciation of mundane activities until we are able to completely detach from samsaric existence. We must also rely upon the accumulation of the two types of merit both by making offerings of our real resources, such as our personal wealth and our body, speech, and mind, as well as by repeatedly making imagined offerings of all that exists in the universe which might be pleasing or helpful to the Three Jewels and all sentient beings without exception. These two types of accumulation of merit allow us to begin building a bridge from samsara into nirvana.

As genuine dharma practitioners we must make and keep dharma commitments with the strongest of samaya, for this allows us to be constantly surrounded by the dharma protectors and the hosts of dakas and dakinis that form an undefeatable army to protect us and conquer the maras that create obstacles for our practice. We must become inseparable from our lama and yidam, for this allows us to be constantly guided through the different bardos, or intermediate states, and ultimately, to be guided into liberation. Finally, we must learn to recognize the true nature of our own mind, which is both empty and luminous, for only this insight will allow us to become liberated from samsara at the moment of our own death.

3.15 Actions of a True Practitioner

The major difference between ordinary beings and spiritual practitioners is one of attitude and motivation—the attitude and motivation that permeate the activities, both positive and negative, of their daily life. Spiritual practitioners perceive not just their suffering, but its cause, and are therefore able to dig up the roots of this suffering and replace them with seeds of positive action.

Spiritual practitioners dedicate their body, speech, and mind to diligently plant such seeds of positivity for the benefit of all sentient beings, not simply their own. Just as someone with a deadly disease would take the prescription for the medicine that cures them, spiritual practitioners take their practice of buddha dharma just as seriously, for it is only the dharma that can save them from the sufferings of samsara. The spiritual practitioner makes a voluntary commitment to practice the dharma for the benefit of all sentient beings without exception, and they view their relationship with these fellow sentient beings like the relationship between a mother and her only child.

Spiritual practitioners first tame their own wild and confused mind so that it becomes peaceful and gentle; it is like taming a wild horse so that, in time, we can ride it swiftly to a desired destination. Spiritual practitioners completely eliminate their one true enemy, ego-clinging, leaving it completely vanquished and destroyed.

3.16 Identifying a Genuine Practitioner

It is easy to differentiate between a genuine practitioner and a nonpractitioner by simply observing his view, meditation, and conduct. As we are involved in dharma practice, changes occur in our view, meditation, and conduct in accordance with the dharma. As a result, we see that we become outwardly stronger while inwardly growing more gentle. By outward strength we are referring to the practitioner's ability to face challenges and turmoil with wisdom and perseverance, yet the inner gentleness allows us to maintain kindness, love, and compassion towards all sentient beings, without exception.

Additionally, the genuine practitioner will fulfill his vows and commitments in accordance with the dharma, and consequently his virtuous prosperity will continue to increase. The true practitioner will find that his perseverance and diligence continue to increase as he dedicates his body, speech, and mind to his dharma practice.

3.17 Selflessness and Compassion

The genuine practitioner practices generosity towards all sentient beings without discrimination and without the hope or expectation of gaining merit. She neither holds desire for samsara nor continues to plant the seeds of cyclic existence. Rather, she digs out the very root of this endless cycle of lives by learning to cherish moral conduct.

The genuine practitioner doesn't allow herself to become overwhelmed by the realization of the number of sentient beings who are suffering in samsara, but instead uses this knowledge to fuel her loving-kindness and compassion towards all sentient beings. The genuine practitioner should never allow herself to become complacent or develop a false sense of contentment in her knowledge of dharma practice, but rather should always strive to study and train in meditation so that she can continue to progress through higher and higher levels of realization.

The genuine practitioner should never allow herself to become attached to name, fame, and respect from others; instead, she should use any attainments of realization and understandings of dharma practice to share teachings only for the benefit and liberation of others.

Finally, the genuine practitioner should never allow herself to fall into a position of bias. Rather, she should maintain perfect equanimity in her kindness and compassion towards all sentient beings without exception. When she has realized her ability to maintain this diligent selflessness and compassionate equanimity, then the power of her precious dharma practice shall know no boundaries in its ability to remove her defilements.

3.18 Cultivating Seeds of Positivity

In order for us to become genuine dharma students, we must first closely examine our own behavior and characteristics. We must cultivate appreciation for the interactions we have with every sentient being we encounter, particularly showing deep kindness and compassion for those with whom we hold a deep connection.

Because all sentient beings have been, at some point since beginningless time, a loving mother, protective father, and generous friend to us, we must remember gratitude at all times and not repay others' kindness in past lives or even this life with negative thoughts, words, and deeds. We only truly become a bodhisattva when, through our loving-kindness and compassion, we are able to view all sentient beings, without exception, as buddhas.

In order to improve our own behavior and characteristics, we should start with the most basic practice—whatever makes us happy and comfortable, whatever brings us pleasure or relieves our suffering, this is exactly what we must do for others. These same causes and conditions are what we should provide for all sentient beings.

Additionally, we can vastly improve our character and activity by maintaining any commitments we have made to our guru and to other sentient beings. Ordinary beings have a tendency to break commitments they make, thus shattering trust and creating obstacles on the path towards enlightenment. However, taking our commitments seriously and following through on them is one of the best ways to improve our character and propel ourselves along the path to liberation.

Also, to make bold improvements in our character we must

be honest and true to ourselves and all other sentient beings by reducing and eventually abandoning any two-faced behaviors we display. Improving our character also requires bringing unshakable focus to the truly helpful and meaningful things in our lives. This includes reducing chit-chat and gossip, which keep us revolving in meaningless circles.

Finally, in order to make improvements to our character and activity, we must cease cultivating the expectation that our wishes of enlightenment will bring us to a fruition without us providing a seed or root; instead, we must plant an abundance of seeds of positivity. Then, through the accumulations of merit and wisdom, we will experience the result in the fruition of our own liberation.

3.19 Living a Wholesome Life

Living a wholesome life requires being able to know which actions of body, speech, and mind bring wholesome results and which actions will cause negative effects. Human existence is precious—it is a great achievement and a great opportunity—for it is the only realm in which we may see the importance of practicing spirituality and acting in accordance with the dharma to live a wholesome and meaningful life.

Through the practice of the sacred dharma in the human realm we can achieve the maximum benefit for both ourselves and others. In fact, it is only by using this precious human existence for practice of the dharma to benefit all sentient beings that we can achieve liberation.

Because dharma practice requires a human birth, we must use this precious opportunity to achieve perfection by living a wholesome life and going beyond love and hate to instead practice with the altruistic mind of the bodhisattva until we have attained liberation.

3.20 The Terror of Ultimate Reality

The genuine Mahayana practitioner knows not only how to find a guru, but also how to maintain the precious connection with the guru throughout his life. The Mahayana practitioner understands the significance of each and every sentient being suffering in the six realms of samsara and, rather than becoming overwhelmed by this understanding and complaining that he cannot help so many suffering beings, he instead expands his practice of bodhichitta to include all of these beings without discrimination. The Mahayana practitioner never allows himself to become prideful or arrogant upon attainment of realization that others may have yet to experience. When most dharma practitioners hear teachings on the nature of ultimate reality and the absence of inherent existence, they cannot comprehend those teachings and may even become terrified; however, the Mahayana practitioner, upon hearing the ultimate teachings, will experience great joy and a sense of comfort as though he is returning home after being away for a long, long time.

3.21 Importance of Constant Reminders

On our spiritual journey as dharma practitioners, it is extremely important that we encounter constant reminders to keep us on track. These frequent reminders should direct and focus our minds on the importance of practice. Without such reminders we will be unable to maintain a steady course on the highway of our spiritual path.

One such reminder is the truth of the impermanence of this lifetime in the human realm. When we realize just how short this lifetime is and that it could end at any time, we feel a sense of urgency and can more easily spend our time and energy on positive activities of ultimate benefit, as opposed to activities that are unnecessary or even negative in nature or effect. It is clear that, when compared to our infinite lives since beginningless time, this life is extremely short, and there are no guarantees on how much longer we'll be here. In truth, nothing can protect us from the irrefutable fact that our own death is a certainty.

Another reminder we can use is the recognition of procrastination. When we experience procrastination we should have the awareness to recognize it for what it is and use that recognition as fuel for our practice. As long as we allow ourselves to be numb to, or unaware of, procrastination, then it controls us. We can waste an entire lifetime blindly fumbling around, spending our time and energy on the mundane. However, when we have the presence of mind to recognize procrastination when it occurs, we use our deficiency as a reminder to bring energy and focus back into our practice.

Another important reminder on our spiritual journey is to

understand the necessity of diligence and exertion. The spiritual path we travel as dharma practitioners is a long one, yet it begins with a single step. A single drop of water seems insignificant, yet every individual drop of water is necessary to create an ocean, which is so large it seems beyond the counting of single drops. Just so, our accumulation of merit and wisdom begins with the simple decision to reject the negative and adopt the positive with diligence and exertion one action at a time until we reach the ultimate goal of liberation—the point at which we have accumulated an ocean of wisdom and merit beyond the counting of single actions.

We must also be constantly reminded of our faith and devotion to the buddha dharma. Not only does our faith help at the most basic level by motivating us to practice regularly and to bring the practice into all aspects of our life, but it also helps at the ultimate level because faith and devotion are critical to our attainment of higher levels of realization.

Furthermore, we must constantly remind ourselves to cut the root of confusion and see through the superficial nature of our ordinary experience of reality. We can allow this to lead us into the ultimate truth that is free of the concepts of existence and nonexistence.

The final reminder on which we must rely on our path to liberation is to depend less and less on societal norms and conventions that are a result of the mundane view of relative truth and superficial reality. Instead, we should reach a point at which we rely one hundred percent on the realization of ultimate truth. Ninety-nine percent of the time, most of us rely

3.22 The Power of Altruism

According to the teachings on the guidelines for bodhisattvas, in order to remain on the bodhisattva path we must be of benefit to all sentient beings no matter where we are born. So in order to remain on the bodhisattva path, we must cultivate the purely altruistic mind of bodhichitta by diligently making aspiration prayers. When we are happy because our life is going well, we must immediately recognize that this is a result of the blessings of the power of our bodhichitta practice and diligently continue our efforts in this regard. Conversely, when we are unhappy and depressed because things are not going well and our life seems dark, we must immediately recognize that we are simply experiencing the ripening of our own negative karma, and diligently move forward with our bodhichitta practice by using our own suffering to help us to cultivate compassion for the sufferings of all sentient beings.

As a dharma practitioner, when we become seriously ill we should use the intensity of our pain and suffering to fuel our bodhichitta practice and deepen that practice to much more advanced levels. When we encounter experiences of great suffering through illness, we become more able to identify with and develop compassion for the suffering of all sentient beings that are sick and in pain, and when we become well we are even more able to feel the effectiveness of our practice and our gratitude for the blessings of the buddhas and bodhisattvas.

When we begin to realize that we are getting older and become concerned as we feel the effects of aging in our bodies, we must use this realization to deepen our understanding that this life is not only short and impermanent, but also constantly getting closer and closer to its end. This realization helps to fuel our bodhichitta practice by providing us a sense of urgency to practice the dharma before it's too late to benefit ourselves and others. Finally, as we enter the process of death, we must not be afraid or regretful for how we spent our time in this life, nor should we make excuses or extend blame towards others. Rather, we must diligently increase our practice of bodhichitta so that we accomplish all that we possibly can in our final moments in this lifetime to prepare for the separation of mind and body.

3.23 The Ultimate Antidote

Ultimately, dharma is the only antidote to cure us of our negative emotions. To heal ourselves completely, we must release our desire and attachment to this life and instead dedicate our life to practicing dharma, generating benefits that will come in the life that comes after our death. Dharma becomes the antidote when our diligence and perseverance become inseparable from devotion and faith.

When we've released completely the ego-clinging of our mind, the antidote of dharma can fully cure all of our fears and doubts. The more we allow the medicine of dharma practice to counteract and transform the poisons and negativities, the more we'll find within ourselves the signs of kindness, gentleness, love, and compassion toward others. As we experience these signs within us and attain greater states of realization, we begin to make a transformation to the altruistic mind of a bodhisattva. How quickly we travel the path to liberation and enlightenment is entirely dependent upon how skillfully we apply the antidote of dharma to transform the poison of our negativities at the very moment of their arising into love and compassion toward all sentient beings. We shouldn't fight with our negative emotions as they arise, but use their very energy to transform them into the antidote of dharma practice which will heal us.

These techniques are how we use dharma as the antidote, which we must apply until we are completely cured of all the poisons of negativity present in our body, speech, and mind until liberation is attained.

3.24 The Practical Side of Practice

In order to practice in our daily lives we must take every situation that arises as an opportunity for dharma practice. Rather than becoming attached to positive experiences and avoiding or disliking unpleasant situations, we should use all experiences as fuel for our practice, as an opportunity to grow and deepen our spirituality. In order to accomplish this as practitioners we must change the attitude we have towards both our practice and our negative emotions. Yet we must also change our attitude toward our guru, the buddhas, and bodhisattvas. Changing our attitude is the necessary prerequisite for all other paths and practices, because it creates space for our faith and spirituality to grow.

An analogy which highlights the importance of our attitude in our practice involves a horse cart. The blessings of the buddhas and bodhisattvas are the horse which pulls us along, our practice is the cart which holds us, and our faith and devotion to the dharma are the harness which connects the horse and the cart. Without a harness, having the horse and cart does us no good. However, with a harness to connect the horse and cart, the cart can be pulled along. Just so, as our attitude of faith and devotion increases, our practice is allowed to progress forward smoothly and without obstacles.

The practitioner will feel a deep connection to the Three Jewels, as well as to her deity practice, as long as she has the right attitude and faith toward her practice. This deep connection enabled by the right attitude produces the realization of ultimate truth we are seeking. At this level of practice faith and devotion are so powerful, so unshakable, that every

3.25 Perfection Comes from Practice

For success in a seclusive retreat, we must have a good foundation of knowledge in the fundamental teachings of the buddha dharma. We must have confidence and certainty in what we want to achieve and how, but this confidence and certainty must be based on our own experience and logical reasoning; if it isn't, we are just fooling ourselves. After all, we may have memorized the words of all eighty-four thousand of the Buddha's teachings, but do we know the essence of those teachings? If we do grasp the essence of those teachings, then we will definitely know what stage we're going through, and will possess an awareness of our own upward progression on the spiritual path. We will have a clear understanding of exactly what level we have attained without depending on an outside opinion. Our satisfaction in the luminosity of our own mind will eventually be so great as to be inexpressible with words. However, it is advised that we not fall into either of the extremes—doubt or expectation, good or bad—at this level of the path.

True perfection is earned by sacrificing time and energy with incredible certainty and confidence. Even if it should be at the cost of our very life, we should be prepared to pay anything to achieve liberation. The genuine practitioner receives the ultimate benefit from their practice when they are willing to voluntarily offer their life for the sake of dharma practice. We should never give up our dharma practice, even if faced with the most serious illness or grave disease. Even within the grips of something surely terminal, we should continue to practice and never lose our connection to dharma. In fact, in such a situation an advanced practitioner can increase their practice and cultivate their connection to the dharma more than ever before.

When we know for a fact that our own death is imminent, each moment becomes even more precious and should be dedicated to the practice of the dharma. Even the pain and agony of our ailment become our teacher, our guru, rather than a problem, for day and night it is a reminder that death is coming and practice is precious. At this point our understanding of and connection to the buddha dharma is so strong that the eight worldly dharmas no longer concern us; they are no longer a hindrance and they have no effect whatsoever on us. Because of the new freedom that occurs in this special state of mind, there are no longer any obstacles to our continuous progression along the path.

At this level of practice, the practitioner is so advanced that he or she can maintain the meditative state even during post-meditation, while continuing to exist and function in the or-dinary world. Although only the most advanced practitioners experience the inseparability of meditation and postmedita-tion, this is an amazing accomplishment that we should all strive to achieve. To achieve this state of true realization be-yond adopting and rejecting requires us to exercise diligence and patience. In this state, called "one taste," we reach beyond dualism and see that adopting and rejecting are two sides of the same coin.

4.1 Developing Inner Confidence

We must contemplate and meditate upon the nature of cyclic existence until we have a complete inner confidence in our understanding of it. This contemplation includes meditating completely on the distinction our mind makes between enemies and friends until we have complete confidence that this distinction is artificial and of no essence. Then, with this complete confidence, we can rest in the complete inner confidence of our equanimity towards all sentient beings.

This contemplation includes meditation upon our every action, including every breath and step we take, until we can come to rest in the complete inner confidence that these actions are completely wholesome and altruistic.

Throughout this contemplation and meditation we must rid ourselves of judgment and ridicule of others' spiritual beliefs and practices, and instead examine our own practice and come to rest in the inner confidence of the ultimate reality beyond any notions of dualism, of "I" and "other."

We shouldn't be surprised or overwhelmed by signs of improvement in our contemplation or meditation, but shouldn't become attached to these experiences of attainment either. We should simply allow them to increase our growing inner confidence in our practice, and propel us toward a state that is free of distinction between meditation and nonmeditation. We must contemplate and meditate upon our love and compassion for all sentient beings until we develop complete inner confidence in our ability to love them all equally and constantly, unhindered or marred by the dualistic framework of distinction and discrimination. We should contemplate and meditate upon which buddha realm we'll be born into in our next life, and develop complete inner confidence in the reasons why.

4.2 Trust the Buddha Dharma

We must learn to trust ourselves when we practice the doctrines of the Buddha. In time, we come to trust the infallibility of karmic cause and effect and of the interdependence of all actions. We must come to know and trust the importance of the accumulation of merit and wisdom, in the same way we know and trust that even the smallest drops of water falling into a bucket will eventually fill it.

We must learn to trust that our own dharma practice *will* remove our entire jungle of kleshas, much like knowing a raging wildfire can clear an entire forest from the earth. All of our negativities can be swept away by the firestorm of our compassionate wisdom. We must trust that all of our happiness and sadness is completely dependent on, and a result of, our previous karma; when we trust this process we can begin the accumulation of virtuous actions immediately.

No one achieves perfection in anything meaningful the very first time they try; however, we've heard the phrase over and over again that "practice makes perfect." It is true that with multiple repetitions and patience everyone can achieve perfection over time. I don't know of anyone who has sat down to meditate for the very first time and immediately attained enlightenment, but just like the drops of water that we trust will eventually fill our bucket, consistent dharma practice will eventually lead us to liberation.

We must learn to trust the truth of our own karma, for as long as karma exists, ego-clinging also exists—they are completely interdependent. Whenever we examine ourselves and sense some ego-clinging, we know there is still some negative karma left to purify. Likewise, when we experience negative karma, we know there is still some ego-clinging left to uproot.

4.3 Tame Your Ordinary Mind

We can tame our ordinary mind through the practice of contentment. Contentment is one of the seven virtuous treasures of the bodhisattva, for it is the antidote to the poisons of desire and attachment. We should tame our enemies through the taming of our own ordinary mind, for by taming our own mind we tame any and all enemies we could possibly encounter. When our mind has been tamed, we are free of any dualistic notion of friend and enemy, of attachment and aversion.

And we can develop bodhichitta by taming our own ordinary mind. In fact, we can benefit countless sentient beings by taming our own ordinary mind through bodhichitta. We first must tame our ordinary mind in order to experience bliss and receive the blessings and transmissions of the lineage, which are of limitless benefit to countless other sentient beings.

We must tame our ordinary mind so that we can experience emptiness and the luminosity of our own mind, for this is the preparation to be born in Sukhavati, or paradise. And it is essential to tame our own mind by developing the altruistic mind of bodhichitta, which is the cause for the cessation of all pain and suffering. This is true because when we plant the seed of bodhichitta and experience the joyfulness and happiness that is its consequence, the very root of all pain and suffering—namely the ego—has no room to grow and hence loses its ability to survive.

When the sky is permeated with the light of the sun—our love for all sentient beings—there is no fear of falling into darkness and shadow. By taming our own ordinary mind, inner experiences of happiness and sadness, as well as outer appearances both positive and negative, are all recognized for what they are: interdependently-arisen phenomena that are merely reflections of our own ordinary mind.

4.4 Conquer Your Wild Mind

As genuine practitioners of dharma, we must conquer our own wild mind before we can hope to conquer the wild minds of other sentient beings. Conquering the scattered craziness that litters our own wild mind is an important first step, and a prerequisite for many further steps, such as developing the correct view of the dharma, banishing all doubts about our practice, and removing all contradictions between relative and ultimate reality. Inexhaustible patience and determination are what we will attain when our own confused, ordinary mind has been conquered.

Until we have tamed our mind we will continue to experience the law of karmic cause and effect. Trapped in samsara and bound by these laws of karma, we experience not only regret for our inappropriate negative actions of the past, but also the terror that comes with our certainty of the suffering that will come when these negative seeds come to fruition.

The true nature of our mind is buddha nature—completely stainless and nothing short of a perfect purity that shines with a radiance like the sun. However, just as the sun's light and warmth can be temporarily obscured by clouds, dust, and pollution, so too our ordinary mind is obscured by negativities which must be removed by conquering the wild mind. Studying and meditating upon the doctrines of buddha dharma are necessary tools; in fact, they are the only tools we can use to truly tame our own wild mind so that we may travel the path toward liberation.

Conquering our wild mind will make us a suitable vessel to hold the sacred teachings, empowerments, and transmissions in order to liberate all sentient beings from samsara. So this conquering of our own wild mind is essential in order to attain enlightenment and recognize the true nature of our ordinary mind. When we clearly see the nature of our own mind, we are liberated, freed of the bondage created by our own dualism. "I" and "other," "good" and "bad," "right" and "wrong" along with all internal pictures and appearances of external phenomena are mere reflections of our ordinary mind and so this recognition of it spontaneously frees us from these dualisms.

4.5 Wisdom Is the Foundation

From the point of view of the dharma, external and internal phenomena are impermanent, mere appearances of superficial reality. This is poignantly true with regard to the lives of sentient beings, the duration of which is always uncertain. Those fortunate enough to possess the wisdom of this truth know to maximize their time in wholesome pursuits of dharma practice.

The samsaric cycle of life is an ocean of suffering within which no ultimate happiness may ever be found. Those fortunate enough to possess the wisdom to recognize this suffering and its causes will eventually find the path to the cessation of this suffering. In our human realm alone we can see millions of our own kind suffering in ways that are unimaginable and overwhelming to many of us here in the West. Yet the actual number of beings suffering even worse conditions in miserable existences within the six realms is infinite: not countable even by enlightened beings and inconceivable to us ordinary beings. Those that are fortunate enough to possess the wisdom and intelligence to recognize the truth of these conditions of extreme suffering in samsara, rather than being overwhelmed or paralyzed by them, will maximize their time by cultivating the altruistic mind of bodhichitta.

The great lineage of enlightened beings has taught us, over and over, that the source of our connection to the Buddha, dharma, and the sangha is our guru and spiritual master, the lama. Those that are fortunate enough to possess the wisdom to recognize this truth cultivate their devotion to their guru continuously and without interruption until they have reached enlightenment.

There are many that practice the three levels of the Buddha's teachings—Hinayana, Mahayana, and Vajrayana. However, only fortunate ones practice from a foundation of wisdom and intelligence that will lead them to attain enlightenment and liberation.

All practice of buddha dharma functions as purification for the practitioner's body, speech, and mind. However, only those fortunate enough to possess the wisdom to recognize the depth of this truth will realize it to the degree that they are inspired to enter seclusive retreat and practice dharma exclusively for the rest of their lives.

4.6 Method and Wisdom

Here the term "fortunate ones" refers to those dharma practitioners who are able to integrate method and wisdom into their practice in order to achieve higher and higher levels of realization.

The ultimate view is beyond fabrication; the fortunate ones are able to maintain the undistracted, or one-pointed, concentration of buddha mind while in meditation. This is a result of their integration of method and wisdom.

The ultimate meditation is the inseparability of emptiness and luminosity; the fortunate ones are able to meditate upon their own mind with unwavering mindfulness and awareness. This is a result of their integration of method and wisdom.

The ultimate conduct is detachment from the appearances of samsara; the fortunate ones have the realization of emptiness of the appearances of samsara and are unattached to them. This is a result of their integration of method and wisdom.

The ultimate fruition is tathagatagarbha; the fortunate ones recognize that this seemingly spontaneous fruition is inherent and inseparable from their own mind. They recognize the basic nature of their mind as buddha nature. This is a result of their integration of method and wisdom.

From the ultimate point of view, the arising, abiding, and ceasing of obstacles and confusions are mere appearances of phenomena. Because these mere appearances are empty of inherent existence, they are self-liberated. However, only the fortunate ones achieve realization of this truth through their integration of method and wisdom.

Our own happiness and sorrow are entirely dependent

upon our own mind's view of our external and internal environment. Through the integration of method and wisdom, the fortunate ones recognize the inseparability of the emptiness and luminosity of mind.

4.7 Knowledge without Essence

Without an understanding and realization of the dharma born from practice and direct experience, conceptual knowledge lacks any true essence, regardless of our level of expertise or ability to debate. Regardless of how skillfully we can present the dharma as practitioners, without the realization of experience our knowledge still has no essence. If negative emotion cannot be transformed through dharma practice, then it does not matter how great a meditator a person might be.

Conceptual knowledge is without true essence if we do not, through our dharma practice, develop realization and a sense of renunciation toward the illusory material world. Even living humbly and alone as a monk or nun or in the stark isolation of a secluded retreat cave is of no essence if our mind still struggles with negative emotions. Receiving ordination, making commitments, or taking vows are simply knowledge without essence if there is not proper motivation or if these acts are not undertaken with a sense of the connection with ultimate reality.

Likewise, the cultivation and accumulation of merit through the practice of the six perfections carried out without the proper altruistic attitude and understanding of ultimate reality represent knowledge without essence because it will not free us from the six realms of cyclic existence.

4.8 Unnecessary Practice

It is unnecessary for us to abandon ordinary society and enter a nunnery or monastery to practice the buddha dharma, as long as our wisdom and our practice continue to increase and we are strong enough that we are able to practice no matter where we live.

It is unnecessary to abandon cyclic existence and become an ascetic or renunciant, as long as our afflictive emotions have become self-liberating due to our mind's ability to rest in the natural state.

It is unnecessary for us to watch and judge other sentient beings experiencing the suffering of confusion and afflictive emotion; instead we must examine the confusion and afflictive emotions that arise in our own mind streams.

It is unnecessary to spend our time immersed in reading countless texts on the buddha dharma, as long as we can recognize and realize the fundamental nature of our own mind.

It is unnecessary to practice renunciation of external and internal phenomena, as long as we recognize all appearances as dependently-arisen illusions, like a dream or mirage.

Finally, it is unnecessary for us to continue to search for Buddha, as long as we attain the realization of ultimate truth ourselves.

5.1 Finding Spiritual Friends

When the time comes that we find a spiritual friend, or guru, to guide us on our spiritual path, it is due to a ripening of positive karma. We need this teacher to escape the cyclic existence of samsara. When we try to traverse the path on our own, without the transmission of teachings from a lineage holder, exploring the realm of spirituality is like wandering in circles throughout a dark and unfamiliar house in which all the exit doors have been locked. With a true teacher to guide us and provide us with the transmission, however, it is as if the lights in the house come on and we are given a key.

The guru is not the only important being to help us along our path. We also find other spiritual friends, the sangha, who are essential to our journey. We receive tremendous encouragement, support, and wisdom from spiritual friends around us who are traveling the same path that we wish to take. Advanced practitioners in particular play a very important role as models for us to follow. In our relationship with the sangha, it is important to appreciate each other and practice the six paramitas, or six perfections. Our appreciation should allow us to learn from spiritual friends, and not fall into negative, judgmental, or biased states of mind.

5.2 Giving Rise to Certainty

Certainty begins to arise when we receive the blessings and inner transmissions from our guru. Uncertainty is dispersed and replaced with certainty when we receive the blessings and siddhis from our yidam deity practice. And certainty arises when we develop a connection with the lama, the deity, and the yidam practice, for these connections remove all obstacles on the path of liberation.

We give rise to certainty by practicing diligently, and by planting this seed of enlightenment the fruition of realization arises spontaneously. Certainty in ultimate reality arises when we practice in relative reality by removing the two types of obscurations or defilements. Ultimately, it is certain that the samadhi of one-pointed meditation brings the experience of a variety of wisdom and realizations.

5.3 Finding the Path to Liberation

It isn't only our spiritual friends, the buddhas and bodhi-sattvas, who show us this path of liberation. If we listen carefully and properly to the teachings, we hear that every sentient being we encounter, every other being we interact with, can show us this path. In short, every moment and every action is an opportunity to practice the dharma.

When we receive teachings from our guru, we get the maximum benefit from those teachings when we possess a pure attitude toward the buddha dharma that is being given by the guru. Sacred dharma teachings are extremely important in our life and path; without them we can never escape from the suffering of cyclic existence—we'll continue around and around in meaningless circles. It is useful to appreciate the importance of the sacred teachings through several poetic metaphors.

For example, we should regard them as a light of wisdom which lights our way out of the labyrinth of dark tunnels though which we are wandering. The teachings provide us with a safe path on our life's journey through the suffering and pain of the treacherous territory of samsaric existence, like a lifeline we can hold on to when we have lost our footing while crossing the torrents of our samsaric lives toward the shore of liberation. The sacred teachings also cut through the ropes of ego-clinging that bind us to samsara, thus allowing us to find the freedom of action to move towards liberation. While the suffering of samsara pulls us down like quicksand, the sacred teachings are a hand that pulls us out and onto dry land. Finally, the sacred teachings are a hammer of wisdom to break the chains of dualism, of subject and object, perceiver and perceived.

Therefore, no matter which of these beautiful analogies we use, we see how essential the role of the spiritual master, or lama, is; without the guru, the teachings cannot be transmitted to us.

5.4 Unmistakable Benefits from the Path

In order to gain a true understanding of the essence of the sacred teachings, we must make a connection with a lama or guru. This connection enables us to receive the transmission of the teachings of our lineage of practice from the lama or guru. To attain realization we must also have meditation experiences that are dependent upon our faith and devotion. This is unmistakable. Realization also depends on our ability or skill in maintaining dharma practice throughout all activity, day and night. This implies we should maintain our practice not only in formal meditation, but in postmeditation as well.

We must plant the seed that will enable us to choose our next birth in a preferred realm of existence rather than simply be swept away by the tide of karmic cause and effect into whatever might await us. To do this, we should practice detachment from both internal and external existence, including all physical, material existence. Make no mistake—while attachment exists, whether internal or external, liberation is impossible.

If we can weave the sacred teachings of sutra and tantra inseparably into the very fabric of our minds, we can follow the path of dharma to its ultimate, unmistakable benefit: liberation.

5.5 Recognition and Understanding

Being adorned with great faith and devotion, although necessary, is not enough to achieve liberation from samsara. We must also have recognition and understanding of suffering and its causes. When we truly recognize and understand the suffering of sentient beings, we become able to spontaneously and selflessly dedicate ourselves to altruistic action to alleviate that suffering.

Also, through recognition and understanding of the illusory nature of the projections of samsara, we increase our level of realization and develop detachment from the mere appearances of arising and ceasing sense phenomena. When we combine our faith and devotion with recognition and understanding of the importance and profundity of the lama's teachings, we begin to hear those teachings at a new, deeper level which brings greater benefit to the development of our realization.

When the seed of faith and devotion grows to the fruition of recognition and understanding, we can finally dig up the three roots of our afflictive emotions—the accumulation of negative karma from unwholesome actions of body, speech, and mind. The combination of faith and devotion is the only way to develop the recognition and understanding of the wholesome or unwholesome nature of our own conduct. The only way to bring the entirety of our conduct of body, speech, and mind in line with true purity of action is to first recognize and understand the nature of that conduct; such recognition and understanding are not possible without pure faith and devotion.

Finally, true recognition and understanding of the nature of our own mind is completely dependent upon the connection of pure faith and devotion. To recognize and understand the true nature of our own mind is to realize our own ultimate buddha nature.

5.6 Respect and Devotion

It is essential that we have respect and devotion for our own lama when we are following the path of liberation. For us as students of the dharma, the lama, or guru, plays a role similar to that of a doctor for a sick person. In order to purify our negative karma, we need a holy lama who can help us by teaching us to remove the root of our karmic disease.

And in order to progress on our path towards liberation, we need the help of the sangha, just as the sick patient needs not just doctors, but also nurses and other hospital staff.

Yet the most essential part of the dharma is the actual practice, which is like the patient taking the medicine that the doctor has prescribed in order to cure our disease.

So within this metaphor, the dharma practitioner is the sick patient, and the lama is the doctor who prescribes medicine in the form of teachings on specific dharma practices, and who eventually leads us out of the misery, pain, and suffering of samsara and into the liberation of enlightenment. At the point of enlightenment, we have reached the ultimate perfection and are completely healed of all sickness.

6.1 Stepping onto the Advanced Path

The advanced practitioner relies upon his or her own altruistic mind and fundamental wisdom rather than the intellectualized concepts created by ordinary sentient beings. In other words, practitioners of this level are much more closely associated with the ultimate truth and yidam practice rather than with conceptual notions of relative reality: they know and understand the nature of relative truth and no longer depend upon it to interpret their world or the nature of their minds.

At this point in our own path we have reached a level where anything and everything we do is dharma practice, whether or not it is perceived as such by ordinary sentient beings. As yogis or yoginis at this level of practice we might wander from place to place with no attachment to a permanent home, wearing only our tummo (inner heat) as clothing, and eating samadhi itself as food—this represents our continually increasing dharma practice.

As yogis and yoginis at this level of practice we embody a level of confidence and devotion to our practice that is unimaginable to the mind of an ordinary person. The sacred, secret practices we undertake are kept secret, because to the ordinary sentient being they might seem to contradict or conflict with ordinary notions of right and wrong or true and false. This is the reason why it can be so difficult for beginning practitioners to grasp certain facets of dharma. This highest level of practice is where we experience the luminosity of bodhichitta and the bliss of unobstructed emptiness which mingles

6.2 Attributes of the Advanced Practitioner

An advanced practitioner has no desire for or attachment to cyclic existence. For her, samsara is like a broken-down car rusting in a junkyard; it is a vehicle that will get her nowhere. Or she might see cyclic existence as one gigantic cemetery; a place of death and decay where we wouldn't want to live, but escape from through the gate to nirvana.

The bodhichitta of an advanced practitioner is so overwhelming toward each and every sentient being, without exception, that it mirrors the love of a mother for her only child. The compassionate wisdom of the advanced practitioner grows with the lush spontaneity of wild flowers carpeting the fields in springtime. The barren fields of winter represent the hearts and minds of all sentient beings, while the advanced practitioner's bodhichitta is like the warming sun and nourishing rains of spring.

An advanced practitioner's diligence and perseverance are so tremendous that no obstacle stands the slightest chance of blocking his path of development; his dedication cuts through obstacles with the ease of a sword slicing a piece of fruit. At this level of practice, our delusions are self-liberated—as if we realize that the snake in the corner, coiled and ready to strike, is actually a piece of rope, lying there innocuously until we need to use it.

At this point we begin to realize more and more our own mind's buddha nature. We may experience this to such a degree that our experience of life and the satisfaction of our attainment are that of reaching into Sukhavati. Our experience of the bliss of perfect purity is like an arrival in paradise.

These are indications that we have moved onto the level of the truly advanced practitioner.

6.3 Right View of the Phenomenal World

We must rid ourselves of attachment and clinging to the phenomenal world, for everything is impermanent and constantly changing as certainly as the four seasons of the year. We should not become attached to this life as though it were permanent, for life is actually both extremely uncertain and terribly short—it is said each of us is like a drop of morning dew on a blade of grass that vanishes with the rising of the sun.

We must not be confused and doubt the cause and effect of our own karma, but instead examine the interdependent causal conditions of all phenomena. For example, we know that planting a specific kind of seed will yield a very specific fruit, and we are never surprised by this result. Likewise, we should develop such certainty that our own actions will yield results that are just as specific and predictable.

Let's not become confused by the artificial distinction between the mind and thoughts or appearances within the mind; they simply coexist in interdependence, like a dream. Without the mind, there is no dream, nor any appearance within the dream.

Let's also eliminate confusion between relative truth and the ultimate truth, for they are inseparable, of one taste, like the reflection of the moon on water. With no moon in the sky, there can be no appearance of the moon in the water, and without the water, there is no place for the moon to appear as a reflection.

It is difficult to describe the experience of "one taste." It is similar to trying to describe the essence of an ice cream flavor to someone who has never tasted anything sweet or creamy—

in short, it is impossible. However, we can say that the realization of one taste is such that we can live in a world where we perceive both apparent and ultimate reality, without adoption or rejection of either view, and walk a middle path between the two extremes. This is the experience of one taste. When we look at the phenomenal world, we must not fall into a false duality of seeing "I" and "other" as two separate entities. It is a bit like making some contrived distinction between the essence of ice and water. Just as there is no ice that is not water, nor water that cannot be frozen into ice, so there is similarly no distinction between what we perceive as "I" and "other." The distinction between "I" and "other" exists completely and utterly interdependently, for without this "I" to be the perceiver, there can be no perceived in the mind, no "other."

6.4 You Are Confused

The reason that any sentient being caught in the cyclic existence of samsara is confused is because of a deluded notion of reality. The deluded mind confuses relative appearances with ultimate reality, but ultimate reality is beyond the perception of the confused, relative mind. Until we recognize our own mind, harmful disturbances will never cease. The appearance of these harmful and negative experiences is none other than the impurity that results from not knowing our own mind.

For instance, when others speak harshly to us or about us, we can get terribly upset, yet the words spoken are merely sound vibrations that float for an instant through the air and then disappear. Grasping on to these words is like chasing an echo. Adopting or rejecting while contemplating whether an idea is good or bad, positive or negative brings us temporary happiness or sorrow. This temporary happiness or sorrow is part of relative truth, and it is very uncertain how long it will last. Negative emotions like anger and hate burn at our basic goodness and further obscure our ability to grasp ultimate reality.

6.5 Illusion without Essence

Although the external phenomenal world appears to exist, it is actually an illusion without real essence, born from the minds of sentient beings. Appearances in the phenomenal world are illusory because they are impermanent; they are constantly changing, like the bubbles that form on the surface of a lake during a hard rain. They disappear as quickly as we can observe them. From an ultimate point of view, the more we investigate appearances in the phenomenal world the more confidence we have in our realization that they are without essence.

We find an excellent example within the natural world in the banana tree. As you peel away the outer layer of bark, you find underneath another layer which, when peeled itself, reveals yet another layer of the same, and on and on until you reach the final, inner layer and unroll it to find it hollow— completely empty! You have to conclude that there was nothing underneath the bark at all, no tree whatsoever. Just so, when we analyze any externally appearing phenomena, no matter how resolutely we try to locate a core that is truly self-existent, not made of smaller parts, not depending on coordinating pieces for its existence, we fail to find anything that is permanent or self-existent. From the standpoint of ultimate reality, all phenomenal appearances are merely illusions; they do not exist because their nature is emptiness. However, phenomena do appear to arise into existence within the minds of sentient beings and we sentient beings become attached to them as if they were real. So these phenomena appear to arise yet are actually illusion without essence, like mirages or dreams — how incredibly amazing!

So if this life is no more real than last night's dream, why do we experience it as so real? Why are we unable to wake from this dream into the liberation of enlightenment? As sentient beings trapped in the cyclic existence of samsara, we develop certain habitual tendencies and patterns—not just ways of behaving, but also likes and dislikes, desires, attachments, and aversions. Just as we carry these patterns into the dream state and behave in predictable ways—avoiding things we dislike and working to acquire that which pleases us—so too we carry these habitual patterns into our next lives, and each time we act from these desires, attachments, and aversions, we only accumulate more and more of this similar karma, so lifetime after lifetime we reinforce these habitual tendencies.

This illusory, dreamlike life is impermanent, constantly changing, and we perceive the forces of change when major events, such as the death of another being, occur in our lives. But an event such as death is not "sudden" at all, and in fact has been racing toward us since the moment we took birth. We know electrons are constantly spinning around the nucleus of the atoms that make up our perceived existence and cellular activity is constant in the bodies of all living things. So, it would be safe to say that although we are not always aware of life's impermanence, change does occur in this existence with the speed of a lightning bolt's flash across the sky. Recognizing that the superficial appearances of relative truth are illusion without essence is the first step on the journey of liberation.

6.6 Transform Your Deluded Mind

We must embrace negative emotions at the time they arise in our mind and transform them by cultivating an altruistic mind. Without the practice of altruism, it is impossible to transform the deluded mind to buddha mind. We must embrace an attitude of loving-kindness and compassion towards all living beings just as if they were our own mother or father. If your particular experience with your own mother or father is not the best example of love and compassion, just think of the one person you love the most in this world, and learn to love all beings in this way without bias or discrimination. We must learn to detach ourselves from our delusion of superficial reality, for as long as this attachment to appearances persists, our suffering will continue and the transformation to a buddha mind is made impossible. The root of our fundamental delusion is our very own mind. Without recognizing the nature of mind itself, it is impossible to uproot this deluded state.

We can transform all obstacles and afflictive emotions as we make our way along the path of liberation. Adverse circumstances that arise in our lives should be seen as teachings and blessings, as opportunities to practice and learn. In this light, negative situations are no longer hindrances, but have become fuel for our transformation to buddha mind.

Absence of distraction is the best kind of meditation, for if there is the slightest distraction, there is no meditation. The perfect meditation is the ordinary mind completely relaxed in its natural state of clarity, luminosity, and emptiness.

6.7 The Common Sense of Balance

When we are deeply involved in the practice of the buddha dharma, the sages advise that we practice a common sense of balance by learning to structure our mundane activities and dharma practice in ways that allow us success in both areas of our life. We should not fall into extremes; neither of procrastinating in our dharma practice with the excuse of mundane distractions, nor of allowing our mundane world to fall apart around us due to an overemphasis on dharma practice which ignores our mundane responsibilities.

Developing this sense of balance between worldly responsibilities and our spiritual practice of detachment is extremely important—without it, we fail. For instance, deciding what to eat and what to avoid, as well as how much to eat and when to stop, and choosing what is healthy or unhealthy for us requires a sense of balance as long as we are dealing with the relative truth of the conditional world. Just as meditation requires an understanding of the practice as well as a determination to carry it out, likewise it requires a sense of balance to determine when to push ourselves harder and when to step back and relax where we are, without falling into either of two extremes. It can actually become an obstacle when we lose our sense of balance; practicing dharma day and night with no recognition of relative reality or fasting for days only to overeat the following week. It is extremely important that we use common sense to avoid extremes and find balance within the mundane world. This includes recognizing that for everyone around us, daytime is daytime and night is night. And we must acknowledge that balanced eating is what is best for our body. We must find the balance within the conditional world or relative truth in order to achieve the ultimate realization, for relative truth depends upon ultimate truth.

6.8 The Spark of Realization

When we see the first spark of realization it is a sign of major improvement in our meditation. We must not confuse apparent reality with ultimate reality and the spark of realization involves transcending the confusion between these two extremes. And we should not be confused by the extremes of eternalism and nihilism, but instead go beyond this confusion to find the middle way—this is also the spark of realization. We must practice the Mahayana, the altruistic mind of bodhichitta, which is unconditional love that is inseparable from emptiness. When we have achieved this unification of indiscriminate compassion and emptiness, we will see the spark of realization.

So, in order to attain the spark of realization we must go beyond the extremes of mental dullness and scattered distraction. Instead we can relax into the natural state of our ordinary mind's luminosity, clarity, and unobstructed spaciousness. The spark of realization will continue to increase with the practice of unifying relative and ultimate truth. We must learn to practice without falling into the two extremes and avoid the dualistic view of relative reality as separate from ultimate reality; we must cease to view them as separate realities and instead embrace their oneness, accepting them as one taste. Eventually we can move beyond even that into the emptiness of all realities, to the truth of dharmakaya.

To attain the spark of realization we must practice the dharma without allowing ourselves to be distracted by the appearance of phenomena or by becoming attached to the idea of phenomena's inherent existence. As we become skillful and learned dharma practitioners, we are like a patient who, although sick, has the knowledge necessary to take the appropriate medicine prescribed by the doctor and thus become well. We as practitioners must execute the practices that our teachers have given us so that we may create the spark of realization that will start the universal fire—the fire that will purify all negativities, transforming them into wholesome, virtuous actions.

So, in order to create this spark of realization that will start the universal fire we must learn, train, and practice, for only through practice is the perfection of our wisdom attained.

6.9 Relative and Ultimate: Inseparable

Spiritual practitioners can be extremely diligent in their dharma practice and yet not experience ultimate success unless they have overcome the desire for and attachment to the mundane world. We can collect large quantities of knowledge and skills throughout our life, but will not attain ultimate benefit from these attainments until we attain the wisdom that cuts through the dualistic mind.

We may even attain many experiences of realization throughout the course of our life, but we will not attain the ultimate realization until we understand the ultimate nature of genuine reality. As spiritual practitioners we may learn much throughout our lives about what positive attitudes and behaviors to adopt and what negative ones to reject, but we cannot attain the ultimate point of view until we achieve the ultimate realization of selflessness.

Finally, as spiritual practitioners we may experience much tranquility, clarity, and joy through our deep state of absorption, but we are not masters until we have attained the unshakable state of mindfulness and awareness of the buddha mind.

6.10 The Superior Path

It is superior to realize the ultimate essence of reality, for it releases us from having to study so many things at the conceptual level. It is superior to dig out the very root of afflictive emotions, for it releases us from having to spend so much time in contemplation. It is superior to realize the ultimate transcendent wisdom, for it releases us from having to depend upon mundane knowledge and methods. It is superior to attain an inseparable connection between one's own mind and the dharma, for it releases us from having to seek blessings from external sources. It is superior to realize the emptiness of birth and death, for it releases us from the cycle of samsara, and it becomes unnecessary to seek any higher attainments. It is superior to realize our own inner buddha nature, knowing that nothing needs to be added or taken away and we have been perfectly pure since beginningless time, for it releases us from having to seek enlightenment from external sources. Finally, when the fortunate ones attain these superior realizations, they also come to the realization that the attainment of buddhahood itself is in their own hands.

6.11 Crucial Factors of Practice

We must remain focused on the most crucial factors of our dharma practice as we continue on our path towards liberation. One of these crucial factors is the renunciation of the dualistic view, utilizing the dharma practice of focusing inward until we are able to completely give up any notion of "I" and "other," thus moving us closer to the goal of liberation. The second of these crucial factors is learning to how to focus outward by utilizing the dharma practice of seeing how the outward appearances of all phenomena are transformed into dharmakaya.

Another crucial factor of our dharma practice is experiencing the waves of the mind's rising and ceasing thoughts and emotions, whether negative or positive. Even though to a beginning student these may at first seem to be obstacles, to the advanced student they are actually a gift, for these waves give us something to work with and transform, and they ultimately provide fuel for our practice.

Additionally, it is also crucial that we use our wisdom to learn and understand the view of ultimate reality while we are on our journey towards liberation. It is also crucial that we use our compassion to create and maintain a connection to the sentient beings struggling and suffering in the relative reality of samsara. Between these two, wisdom and compassion, we must use our one-pointed intense concentration to create a meditative absorption that is unshakable and unbreakable. If we can integrate each of these crucial factors into our dharma practice, then there is no doubt that we will truly find the path of liberation.

6.12 Detach from Phenomena Arising

We must detach from the projections of internal and external phenomena in order to succeed in our journey towards our goal of liberation. We must detach from futile searches for external sources of buddha nature; rather, you must look inward and recognize that the basic goodness of buddha nature is only to be found within yourself. As true meditators we must detach from speculation and understanding at the intellectual level; rather, you should look inward to experience the understanding of ultimate reality that can only result from meditation. We must detach from the outer appearances of the projections of external phenomena, and instead realize that all phenomena are dependently arisen and empty of inherent existence. We must detach from notions of happiness and sorrow; in fact, you must detach yourself from all notions of positive and negative emotion, and rather discover your own buddha nature, which is beyond any construct of positive or negative emotion. We must detach from the illusory projection of our own negative karma, for if you are deceived by these projections, you are obscured and therefore unable to see the true nature of ultimate reality. Finally, the true practitioner knows how to detach from all of these obstacles and obscurations in order to remain and move forward on the path of ultimate liberation.

7.1 Guard against Degeneration of the Dharma

In this fortunate eon, the light of the buddha dharma is just beginning to truly dawn; enlightened society has only begun to arise. However, there are many activities of body, speech, and mind that cause the dharma to degenerate: looking down upon and disrespecting beings that are less fortunate; showing disrespect towards the buddhas and bodhisattvas and their activities; and spreading one's own confused theories and wrong views to other sentient beings as well as making those flawed ideas seem to be as important as the sacred dharma.

The less we connect with all other sentient beings through bodhichitta, the further we are from the liberation of buddhahood. When we delude our existence through the vessel of our body and mind, we shift ourselves further and further from liberation. If we wish to keep clean, pure water in a vessel, the vessel itself must be clean! So to cultivate wholesome action, the vessel of our body, speech, and mind must be purified.

According to the Vajrayana teachings, deity practices play an important role in attaining individual liberation. Within the various deity practices of Mantrayana there are several ways of visualizing the deity: visualizing the deity in front of and above you, facing yourself; visualizing the deity above your crown chakra; visualizing yourself as the deity; and visualizing yourself transforming into the deity are all recommended methods. The deity practices are so important because without a strong connection or association to a yidam practice we can face many obstacles along our path to liberation. In short, they are a strong counterforce to the degeneration of the buddha dharma.

Without good direction paired with appropriate action, we will experience dissatisfaction and disappointment in the end. Even if we do have wisdom, lack of the accumulation of merit can cause that wisdom to deteriorate. Lacking wisdom or merit or worse, lacking both, will lead us to rebirth in the three lower realms with an inability to liberate ourselves from the suffering of cyclic existence. These are all aspects of the degeneration of the teachings of the sacred buddha dharma.

7.2 Practice without Reservation

As genuine practitioners of the dharma we must surrender ourselves completely to our practice, relinquishing all doubts, regrets, and resentments in order to practice without reservation.

At the level of our physical body, as we move through our dharma practice we experience many sufferings of pain and discomfort, but we must deal with and let go of these without reservation.

Verbally, we must detach ourselves from idle and meaningless chatter, and instead use our speech for meaningful activities, such as mantra and prayers.

Mentally, we must let go of our mind's ordinary desires and detach ourselves from grasping at the pleasures of mundane distractions and emerge from our aversion towards afflictive emotions, and instead practice the dharma without reservation.

Without reservation, having overcome hesitation and fear, with no regret or resentment, we must become like a child of the mountain who dedicates his body, speech, and mind to dharma practice in seclusive retreat in a cave. While in this retreat we must continue to meditate on samadhi, but without getting sidetracked by obstacles, such as breaking vows of ordination we have taken or breaking other commitments we have made in our practice. If we can follow the guidelines in our practice that are outlined here, then we are truly practicing without reservation.

7.3 Secluded Retreat

As practitioners we eventually reach the point where we can practice alone, in secluded retreat, like masters such as Milarepa, who practiced in isolated mountain caves for years, without interacting with other people, using other practitioners as models, or even having the guru as a guide. At this point we have the confidence to do a retreat which includes not practicing at our teacher's side. You could say we no longer have any questions to ask—it is simply a matter of accomplishing the practice.

For this step we need not only a strong mind with a proper motivation, but also a strong physical body to withstand the rigors of retreat. Yet actual physical weakness is not the only potential obstacle here; simple mental uncertainty regarding our physical ability to succeed in the retreat can be a formidable obstacle to what we are trying to achieve at this higher level of practice.

A thing to remember is that at this point in our progression along the path, our meditation practice increases dramatically, and our worldly activity naturally falls away. To fuel and sustain this increased level of meditative stability and energy, the retreatant must have a large enough supply of dharma practices, including transmissions, teachings, and empowerments, to provide him with plenty of "homework" to do during the years in retreat. Having confidence in the view of Buddhist doctrine is crucial prior to beginning this kind of long-term, intensive retreat.

Choosing the proper location for a secluded retreat has a crucial impact on the prosperity and success during the retreat. The land on which the retreat site is located should be extremely secluded and in a natural setting, such as in the mountains or a forest, and should possess a peaceful, healing energy that is harmonized with the surrounding elements, including the weather and the potential for natural disasters. The location should also be free of harmful beings, whether human or nonhuman. Choosing a cave where others have already practiced and gained spiritual realization is of great benefit.

We should also choose a location in which distractions to our practice are naturally limited and where we are easily accessible to whatever benefactors are providing our supplies throughout the retreat. In terms of dealing with supplies, we should not fall into extremes by eating too much or not eating enough in an attempt to be frugal. In order to accumulate merit, we should have enough provisions to make offerings to the Buddha, dharma, and sangha.

In order to continually deepen our understanding during retreat, reading sacred texts and learning new techniques for practice are necessary. We should always be prepared to face obstacles and challenges that will undoubtedly arise during this retreat; we should never expect that everything will always be easy and full of glory and splendor. We will not have access to the conveniences, luxuries, and comforts of modern life, and we should be prepared to let go of material pursuits, including name, fame, and power.

Although we forgo contact with friends from our regular mundane life while in retreat, we will discover and become deeply acquainted with a new group of friends that will help our wisdom and compassion flourish and prosper. These "friends" will be a new external strength coupled with an internal sense of peace and harmony. Remember that increased confidence, perseverance, and wisdom are the very goal of this retreat; without them all the work and sacrifice is meaningless.

We must develop the ability to harmonize and apply our practice to whatever situation occurs. And as the arrogance and conceit that result from ego-clinging begin to diminish, our body, speech, and mind begin to naturally harmonize. At this point we are able to learn in a much truer sense, let go of our dualistic notions of reality, and gain some greater realization. Our six senses begin to harmonize as well and as this harmonization builds our strength of mind, our practice deepens and strengthens even more. The deep sense of tranquility we gain causes our senses to harmonize, which will increase our inner strength dramatically. At this level of practice we are able to continually increase our samaya, or commitments, in strict adherence because our inner confidence is growing at an accelerated rate. In addition, our bodhichitta, our loving-kindness and compassion toward all sentient beings, begins to flow forth from us in a different, much greater way than ever before. As this new altruistic state of mind increases, our understanding of buddha dharma also reaches new heights. We begin to realize our deep connection with all other countless sentient beings, and as this realization of interconnection deepens it reinforces our growing bodhichitta. Without this loving-kindness and compassion, our practice cannot grow to the levels necessary for attainment of buddhahood.

SARVA MANGALAM!

Glossary of Terms

Arhat: "The worthy one" *(Skt.)*, who has reached the highest level of the Hinayana.

Bardo: "In-between state" *(Tib.)*. In the Vajrayana, six in-between states are defined: the bardo of birth, the dream bardo, the bardo of meditation, the bardo of the moment of death, the bardo of ultimate reality, and the bardo of becoming (rebirth).

Bhumi: "Land" *(Skt.)*, that is the ten stages through which a bodhisattva must pass to attain buddhahood.

Bodhisattva: "Enlightenment being" *(Skt.)*, a being who seeks buddhahood for the benefit of all through the practice of the perfections of virtue but who renounces personal liberation until all samsara has been emptied.

Buddha: "The Awakened One" *(Skt.)*, a being completely released from the cycle of existence into transcendent omniscience.

Dharmakaya: "Body of great order" *(Skt.)* or true nature of a buddha, united with the very essence of the universe (see *Three Kayas*).

Guru Rinpoche: "Precious Teacher" *(Tib.)*, appellation reserved for the great eighth-century master Padmasambhava, who is regarded as a second Buddha, founder of Buddhism in Tibet.

Hinayana: "Small Vehicle" *(Skt.)*, teachings of the first traditions that developed between the death of the historical

Buddha Shakyamuni and the end of the first century B.C.E. which posit nirvana and personal liberation as the ultimate goal.

Kagyu: "Oral Transmission (Lineage)" *(Tib.)*, one of the four principal living schools of Tibetan Buddhism, founded by Marpa, who brought the transmissions of the Indian sages Tilopa and Naropa to Tibet in the eleventh century.

Karma: "Action" *(Skt.)*, the volitional fruit of the universal law of cause and effect; that which engenders rebirth or liberation based upon intention.

Karmapa: "Buddha activity (man)" *(Skt. & Tib.)*, the supreme head of the Kagyu School, embodiment of compassion and wisdom, currently in his seventeenth incarnation.

Klesha: "Trouble, defilement, craving" *(Skt.)*, an unwholesome quality that dulls the mental faculties and engenders negative karma.

Mahasiddhi: "Great blessings," *(Skt.)* derived from **Mahasiddha**, i.e., "Great master of perfections," a being who has achieved perfect individual realization and has thereby attained visible signs of having many blessings and abilities.

Mahayana: "Great Vehicle" *(Skt.)*, teachings of the second group of traditions that developed in the first century C.E., in which the intention is the welfare and ultimate liberation of all beings.

Mandala: "Circle, arch, ovoid" *(Skt.)*, symbolic representation of the cosmos, also of the body, speech, and mind of the buddhas, used as a support for meditation when in diagrammatic or pictorial form.

Mara(s): "Murder, destruction" *(Skt.)*, designated after the name of the lord of the sixth heaven of the desire realm, symbolizing the kleshas or defilements which attack the practitioner seeking to achieve liberation.

Milarepa: "Mila the cotton-clad" *(Tib.)*, the most famous poet-sage of Tibet; spiritual heir of Marpa and composer of spontaneous songs of realization (dohas). Milarepa (1025-1135), after accumulating much evil karma, was able through great ascetic discipline and effort to overcome all obstacles and to reach enlightenment in a single lifetime.

Nirmanakaya: "Body of transformation" *(Skt.)*, the earthly body in which buddhas appear in order to guide other beings to liberation (see *Three Kayas*).

Nirvana: "Extinction" *(Skt.)*, i.e., of the fires of desire, greed, and ignorance; the final goal of Hinayana; freedom from rebirth; absence of arising, changing, or passing away.

Preta: "Departed one" *(Skt.)*, often translated as "hungry ghost," these are beings whose karma is not quite evil enough for hell but is not nearly good enough for any more fortunate rebirth. Pretas are often depicted as having immense bellies and tiny mouths which result from a lack of generosity in previous existences.

Samadhi: "Made firm, established" *(Skt.)* is the term applied to a nondualistic meditative absorption (one-pointed meditation) that is free from both attachment and effort.

Sambhogakaya: "Body of delight" *(Skt.)*, the subtle body of buddhas in buddha realms (or paradises) enjoying the enlightened delights of truth.

Samsara: "Journeying" *(Skt.)*, the cycle of existence, a succession of rebirths that is conditioned by the three unwholesome roots (desire, greed, and ignorance). Samsara conventionally is depicted as having six realms: hells, hungry ghost realm, animal kingdom, human realm, jealous god domains, and god realms, through which beings endlessly cycle until they attain realization.

Sangha: "Crowd, community" *(Skt.)*, the beings who keep alive the teachings of the Buddha and constitute one of the Three Jewels; originally, the communities of monks and nuns where buddha dharma was practiced and taught.

Six Realms: Synonym for samsara (see above).

Sutra: "Thread" *(Skt.)*, the discourses of the Buddha, collected in the Tripitaka. These discourses are traditionally ascribed to the efforts of the Buddha's great disciple Ananda, who recited the discourses from memory to the first Buddhist council to assemble at Rajagriha after the Buddha's parinirvana (death). The sutras contain the basic elements of Buddhist practice.

Tantra: "Weft, warp, to stretch without a break" (as in weaving), *(Skt.)*. Like the threads of a loom, tantric ritual practices provide structure for interweaving the myriad elements of the sutras. Tantra also refers to the texts of advanced yogic practices of body, speech, and mind, which together form the Vajrayana path.

Three Jewels: This term refers to the Buddha (the perfect teacher), the dharma (the "way" or the perfect teachings) and the sangha (the noble community). The Three Jewels are the objects of refuge, which means we have confidence that these three can help us to avoid negative rebirths and to gain enlightenment.

Three Kayas: "Kaya" *(Skt.)* means "body" and the three kayas are the bodies of enlightenment: dharmakaya or reality body, the sambhogakaya or archetypal enjoyment body, and the nirmanakaya or created body which manifests in time and space.

Vajrayana: "The Indestructible Vehicle" *(Skt.)*, developed out of Mahayana teachings on wisdom and compassion combined with mystical and ritual yogic methods in which the guidance of an authentic teacher is essential for progress on the path.

Yidam: "Firm mind" *(Tib.)* is the Vajrayana term for a personal "deity" whose nature, manifested in meditation, corresponds to the temperamental essence of the practitioner. Yidams are models for behavior (such as the bodhisattvas); also each yidam indicates a personal commitment, a practitioner's choice to become a stream-enterer and to reach enlightenment for the benefit of all beings.

Acknowledgments

There are a few individuals without whom this text would never have come into existence to continue the turning of the dharma wheel. I wish to thank these people for helping to bring this project to completion for the benefit of all sentient beings:

Aaron Price, for the initial translating and writing, as well as organization and design;

Ben Koch, for initial editing, and his family, for their patience and support of his efforts in my favor;

Linda Sperling, for even more intense editing as well as painstaking construction of the glossary;

and finally my family, Tashi Chotso and Tashi Dolkar, for their patience and support of this project.

⌘ Dedication

May the buddhas and bodhisattvas grant the power of their compassion that the composition of this text, a blessing from the Three Jewels of Buddhism, makes merit dedicated to the benefit of all sentient beings; may they be liberated without exception.

May the lineage holders and spiritual friends be pervasive like space, and may their presence illuminate the entire universe like the dawning of infinite suns. May their teachings remain like a mountain, forever indestructible.

May the foundation of the buddha dharma be the members of its spiritual community, and may they find not only harmony among themselves, but also energy to constantly increase the three types of wisdom: learning, training, and meditation.

This is the root essence of the buddha dharma.

May the practitioners of the sacred buddha dharma never break their samaya commitments. May they perfect the generation and completion stages of their meditations in their practice of the Vajrayana.

May the dharma protectors continuously watch over and benefit the practitioners to help them to achieve liberation for all sentient beings without exception.

May those kings and ministers who strive to benefit the dharma possess great wisdom and live long, productive lives.

May the sponsors and benefactors of the Buddhist community enjoy an abundance of wealth and an absence of obstacles.

May all communities of all the countries of the world experience harmony and happiness.

May I and all sentient beings on the path of dharma encounter no obstacles to fulfilling our ultimate wish: that I, and all sentient beings with which I have a good or bad connection, achieve the liberation of buddhahood.

Sarva Mangalam!